Er is maar één land: de aarde
één volk: de mens
één geloof: de liefde
— Mardjan Seighali

Thank you, my love.

IF YOU DON'T

ECONOMICS FOR CREATIVE PEOPLE

Co-written & edited by Anne de Bruijn

BIS Publishers

Table of Contents

6

18

64

124

SAVING THE WORLD BY DOING NOTHING

ECONOMICS FOR CREATIVE PEOPLE

Start Here

Pick up your phone and you're immediately hit with bad news. As you doomscroll, one headline after another announces the end of the world. Climate change, pollution, extreme wealth, extreme poverty, political turmoil, loss of biodiversity, food insecurity... it's overwhelming. At the same time, you want to do something about it. But where to start?

The buildings we design, the products we make, the brands we create, the fashion trends we set, the art we craft — they all require resources. That means that, as creative people, we're part of the problems the world is grappling with. Artists, designers, and other creatives often criticize the capitalist system, but let's be real: we depend on it, too. We don't create our art solely for our love of it — it also pays our bills.

So, as a creative person, what exactly is my responsibility in all this? Can I tune out all the news of impending doom, keep calm and carry on creating stuff as always, trusting a solution will present itself? Or do I need to hit the streets in protest? Design a poster about climate change? Should I be standing up against the current economic system? Or try and change it from the inside? How do I even do that when I work in the creative industry? What impact can art and design have?

What you are responsible for is the thing inside your control, indeed the only thing that has ever been inside your control: your mindset.

— Clover Hogan

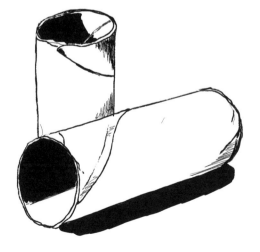

Creativity is Economics

If we want to figure out what we can do for the planet and its future, we first need to imagine what that future might look like. To do that, we have to understand the present. In other words, we must know how we ended up in this situation. That's why this book has 3 parts: From the Past → Into the Present → Towards the Future. We get into natural history, the history of homo sapiens and then we talk about what humans created: the economy. Economics!? Yep, economics. Sometimes it's good to step out of your comfort zone and look at the world from a different angle.

Humbug!
— Ebenezer Scrooge

Why Economics?

Because economics is right at the intersection of all things relevant to what humanity has lived through and created on planet Earth: history, science, social developments, and human society as a whole.

What exactly is economics? What does the word even mean? Originally, 'economics' comes from the Greek 'oikonomia,' a combination of 'oikos', meaning house, estate, or family, and 'nomos', meaning both rule and management. Economics literally means managing a household.

Xenophon, a Greek philosopher who wrote the book 'Oikonomikos' (Economics), posited that economics — or household management — was an art form. Aristotle built on this idea but differentiated between economics (managing the household) and chrematistics, the art of wealth accumulation.

This distinction seems to have disappeared in today's (Western) economy: economics is often understood to be all about wealth accumulation. Our economy is about the market, ruled by the ancient law of supply and demand. In that system, when you can sell something for more than you planned, and the other person can buy it for less than they were willing to pay, both parties benefit. This benefit is often called 'wealth'. Today's society is focused on generating more 'wealth' — producing faster and more. Growth of wealth has become the ultimate goal, which many people have also come to equate with happiness.

> We are, after all, homo economicus.
> — Krina Alizond-114

If you want to grow, you need more resources: labour, time, and knowledge, sure, but also physical resources: raw materials. For a long time, people assumed — and many still do — that these resources are endless, inexhaustible. But they're not. The numerous consequences of 'economic growth' are becoming more and more measurable; things are changing on our planet. That's why we have to make conscious choices about how we create and live. This is where the ToDon'tList method comes in.

The ToDon'tList Method

This book is the third in the 'Don't' series. The first two, 'Don't Read This Book — Time Management for Creative People' (2016) and 'Don't Buy This Book — Entrepreneurship for Creative People' (2020), are about how you make choices in your life, work, projects, and running a studio. This book focuses on the impact these choices have on the world.

In the first 2 books, we use the ToDon'tList method to help with decision-making. It works like this: we're always coming up with new ideas, and there are always things we want and need to do. But trying to do all of these things leads to an ever-growing to-do list. Instead of trying to do as much as possible all at once, you could choose to delete a bunch of to-dos and instead, focus on what really matters. Set boundaries, make choices, do less, but do it better. Because time is a non-renewable resource.

To attain knowledge, add things every day. To attain wisdom, subtract things every day.
— Laozi

The higher up in the decision tree you choose to do or not do something, the bigger the impact on all the to-dos that come after. This choice affects all the resources you need: time, labour, money, and raw materials. For example, if I decide not to bake bread, then I don't need to buy flour, make dough or check the dough's rise either, and I'll have more time to do something else.

This principle works the other way around, too. The choices we make on a daily basis also affect the things that come before it. For instance, if you buy clothes, those garments have been shipped to where you live, constructed by someone, the cotton was grown, etcetera. By making decisions, we affect the economy — how it works and what it focuses on. The same goes for the work you do as a creative: it affects the world you live in. Positively or negatively.

A Hitchhiker's Guide to Earth

Once, economics denoted the art of managing a household. Thinking about the Earth, we could consider Earth our household. It is the 'house' where we all live together — not just us humans, but also animals, plants, and other organisms.

Henry George, an American political economist and journalist, described our Earth as a 'spaceship' in his work 'Progress and Poverty' (1879). This view of the world was echoed by many, among them George Orwell in his book 'The Road to Wigan Pier' (1937): "The world is a raft sailing through space with, potentially, plenty of provisions for everybody; the idea that we must all cooperate and ensure everyone does their fair share of the work and gets their fair share of the provisions seems so blatantly obvious that one would think no one could fail to accept it unless they had some corrupt motive for clinging to the present system."

Even though the idea of Spaceship Earth is about 150 years old, it seems more relevant than ever today.

DECISION TREE

Top Down View

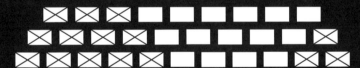

Bottom Up View

We'd be fools not to ride this strange torpedo all the way out to the end.
— Hunter S. Thompson

Saving the World by Doing Nothing

The choices we make, individually or as groups, don't just affect us and others; they ultimately impact Earth too. If we do nothing, our spaceship will no longer be fit for us to travel in sooner or later. The silver lining is that, without us, Earth will be able to heal itself.

If we start doing some things differently or stop doing them altogether, we open up new ways to take care of our spaceship. That way, we can stay here a bit longer. How? That is what we're going to talk about.

> If you think you're too small to make a difference, try spending the night in a closed room with a mosquito.
> — African proverb

Changing the future seems like a huge task. But you already have changed it — without even thinking about it. You have made tons of choices that affect the future. And you can change more things about the future still, even with seemingly small choices.

A meme I found said it quite well: "When people talk about travel to the past, they worry about radically changing the present by doing something small. Few people think that they can radically change the future by doing something small in the present."

I guess you guys aren't ready for that yet…
But your kids are gonna love it. — Marty McFly

Gentle reminder: fear is a bad advisor
In this book, you'll sometimes come across stories and figures that might dishearten you. In those cases, please remember that fear is a poor advisor. If we want to come up with solutions, we need to be brave enough to look the beast in the eye. Let's get going.

Sometimes we are so afraid to be political… But at the end of the day, you are an artist. And an artist's job is to make people uncomfortable.
— Adebayo Oke-Lawal

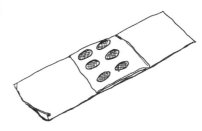

Sun

Place this part at a distance of 46.5 metres

Earth

Moon

·

FROM THE PAST

THE GROUNDWORK

I believe art is an ancient language that we use to communicate with each other into the future.

— Wangechi Mutu

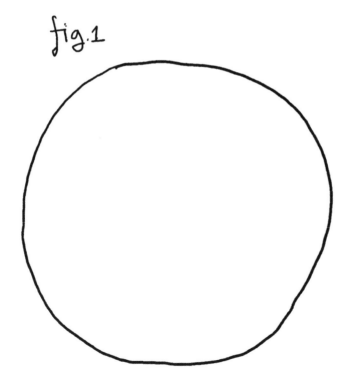

fig.1

A Micro History of Life

KABOOM!!! It's 7,500,000,000 years ago. A massive star dies. A supernova. The gravitational wave it creates — carrying elements like silicon, nickel, and sulphur — shoots out into the universe. After millions of years, this wave hits a cloud of gas, dust, and ice. Gravity makes everything pull together and spin. In the centre, the pressure gets so intense that hydrogen atoms fuse into helium. Heat and light are released, and there she is — completely regenerated — the Sun!

Oh, brilliant!
— Dr. Who

The birth of planet Earth

As the Sun spins, all the elements from the cloud of gas, dust, and ice, along with those from the supernova, form a system of planets. One of these is Earth.

In the beginning, Earth is a mass of swirling lava, bombarded by asteroids, comets, and even other planets. When a planet about the size of Mars crashes into it, two things happen: that planet becomes part of Earth, making it larger — and the force of the impact sends a lot of debris into space. This debris initially forms a ring around Earth until it clumps together and eventually forms the Moon.

Over millions of years, planet Earth slowly cools down. Water vapor in the atmosphere condenses and becomes rain — a downpour that lasts millions of years. The fireball that was Earth is covered by a vast ocean.

Back then, about 4.5 billion years ago, Earth spun much faster on its axis, and the Moon was in a different position in relation to Earth, causing gigantic tsunamis each time there was a high tide. Can you imagine all this happening in the very place where you're reading this book right now?

The metallic core of Earth remained hot and thus liquid. It provides a liveable temperature and a magnetic field that extends far into space, protecting Earth from the harmful radiation and particles emitted by the Sun, the solar wind.

Life creates conditions conducive to life.

— Janine Benyus

The origin of life

About 100 million years after Earth came into being, life would create itself. There are also theories suggesting that life on Earth might have arrived on one or more asteroids that crashed into it — meaning that everything on Earth has an alien origin.

Anyway... Deep in the oceans, single-celled organisms formed as a result of chemical reactions. Researchers from Montana State University discovered that these types of geological processes are still active today.

2.5 billion years later, single-celled organisms started living together within cell membranes, exchanging nutrients and genes. Cells integrated, each taking on a unique function and working in unison. This marked the emergence of a new order of life: eukaryotes, which are capable of reproducing themselves. The exchange of genetic material led to genetic variation and diversity: all fungi, plants, and animals are eukaryotes — from trees to blue whales. In short, as Darwin discovered, all life descends from these first forms of life.[1]

All this is what most scientists currently believe about the origin of life on Earth. But they're still researching and no doubt discovering more.

The first animals

Back then, the amount of oxygen in the atmosphere was less than a tenth of what it is now. But life will always find a way: about 635 million years ago, creatures emerged that could survive on even this limited amount of oxygen: sponges. A sponge is just a mass of cells with thousands of tiny holes, channels, and pores (it has no organs).

Scientists now think that this simple life form contributed to an increase in oxygen. Over millions of years, they filtered dead organic material from the seawater, taking it away from bacteria that would have used a lot of oxygen during digestion.

---

1 → The oldest form of multicellular life dates back to 2100 million years ago.

24 As the amount of organic material in the sea decreased, the light of the Sun could reach deeper layers, which allowed plants to grow. In these now oxygen-rich oceans, various little creatures started to develop.

These tiny creatures had one opening in their bodies that both took in nutrients and expelled waste: a mouth/butt, so to speak. As evolution progressed, some of these creatures developed a digestive tract and thus a separate exit for number twos — they became worms. More and more animals appeared with a front end and a rear end. And, as evolutionary biologist Henry Gee mentions in his book 'A (Very) Short History of Life on Earth,' animals with a front and back tend to move in a specific direction: forward.

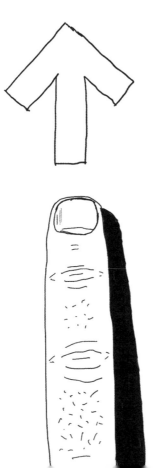

#1

GO FORWARD

Everything is always in motion. Go with that flow, but keep evolving. Adapt to changing circumstances without losing sight of where you want the flow to take you. Make choices that support where you want yourself and the world to go.

N_2

Tiny organisms began producing oxygen (O_2). About 2.75 billion years later, oxygen made up 21% of the atmosphere, and nitrogen (N_2) accounted for 78%. Nitrogen was discovered in 1772 by Scottish chemist Daniel Rutherford. In his experiment, he put a mouse in a jar until it died from lack of oxygen. Then he burned a candle and phosphorus in it, before removing the produced carbon dioxide from the jar with a chemical reaction. He called the remaining gas Noxious Air (N_2). This gas is not 'noxious' for everything and everyone: nitrogen, which it is commonly known as, is an essential nutrient for plants.

No wonder that the first farmers, whose livestock wandered everywhere, realized that their livestock's dung made their plants grow better: it's full of nitrogen. But beware: too much nitrogen creates overly fertile soil, which poses a danger to biodiversity. Plants like grass, brambles, and nettles thrive on nitrogen-rich soil and can overwhelm other plants. These plants, along with the insects that depend on them, will then die off. Insects have 'plant partners' and can't just switch to a different type of plant.

Soil that is too rich in nitrogen also makes trees vulnerable; trees root less deeply in it. But these are not the only consequences of too much nitrogen in the environment. Whenever a plant, tree, or insect disappears, something else always follows; there will be consequences in the food chain's next level every single time.

CO_2

Plants also need carbon dioxide (CO_2), which is made up of carbon and oxygen atoms. Plants use CO_2 in photosynthesis to grow, and in return, they release oxygen. CO_2 makes up about 0.038% of the atmosphere.

CO_2 is produced when carbon (which is found in wood, coal, petroleum, and natural gas, for instance) burns and reacts

ATMOSPHERIC COMPOSITION

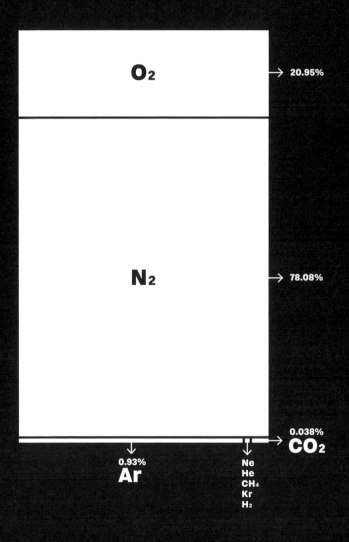

with oxygen. This happens naturally in wildfires and volcanoes, but it's also produced by animals — and humans. We digest food in our bodies and emit CO_2 as a result. And we release extra CO_2 through combustion processes in airplanes, ships, cars, factories, etcetera.

Atmosphere change

Climate change occurs because the composition of the atmosphere is changing. Without the extra emissions, the balance of N_2, O_2, and CO_2 would be just right to allow Earth, with all its life as we know it, to function. With the right amount of CO_2, the atmosphere acts as a pleasant blanket for Earth: part of the Sun's heat, which the planet reflects, stays within the atmosphere. Without CO_2, Earth would cool down to -18°C. With the right CO_2 balance, there is just enough heat to keep Earth at an average temperature of 15°C.

The extra CO_2 that we produce — which cannot be absorbed by trees and plants (because there aren't enough of them) — lingers in the air. The CO_2 blanket thickens, and traps more heat in the atmosphere. This throws things off balance.

Some parts of the world get warmer climates, while others become uninhabitable. The scariest part of this phenomenon is that the process becomes irreversible once you reach certain tipping points. It's like a chair you're leaning back on, teetering back and forth on two legs. Lean too far back, and a fall becomes inevitable.

So — this is the moment to think and act if you want to leave the world habitable for your children and their children (or your nieces and nephews, or your friends' kids).

> **Once you're a parent, you're the ghost of your children's future.** — Joseph A. Cooper

Oil from life

Alongside oxygen, all that primordial life brought about something else: oil. Dead algae, plankton, and bacteria sank to the seabed, which was then covered with sand, stone, etcetera, which exerted tremendous pressure. This pressure and the high temperatures found deeper underground (about 90°C) caused a chemical process that created crude oil. Even higher temperatures resulted in the creation of natural gas.

This process took millions of years, during which the oil and gas also slowly rose upward. The oldest oil (and thus, proof of earliest life on Earth) was discovered in Australia: it is 3.2 billion years old. It is somewhat paradoxical that oil, which originated from the first forms of life, became one of our most important resources, the products of which now threaten life on Earth.

In Between the Ice Ages

Planet Earth is here, the atmosphere is here, the first animals are here, and there are raw materials. But Earth would still change in form and composition many times over. Animals came onto land, started to fly, and sometimes returned to the water (to become whales). The planet would experience catastrophes that destroyed everything. Recovering from such events would take millions of years, but life always returned — even after the ice ages, that could last millions of years. Can you image the entire planet covered in ice?

Ice ages are caused by the amount of solar radiation that reaches Earth (less radiation = temperature drop) and are intensified by long-term mechanisms in the climate system such as the growth of ice caps and the carbon cycle. Milutin Milankovitch, a Serbian engineer and geophysicist, discovered that Earth's orbit around the Sun and the tilt of its axis slowly but predictably vary in cycles of 26,000, 41,000, and 100,000 years. These variations also affect the onset of ice ages.

The last ice age ended about 10,000 years ago. The next one is expected in about 15,000 years. So, the development of modern humanity sits between these two ice ages. If we do the math, that includes the Middle Ages, but also the Roman Empire, ancient Greece, ancient Egypt, the Nabataeans, the Chinese dynasties, the Sumerians in Mesopotamia, the Maya civilisation...

It's no coincidence that our current era is also called the Anthropocene, from the Ancient Greek word anthropos for human. It's the era in which humans are the most influential factor on Earth.

When exactly did the Anthropocene begin? True to human nature, there's debate about that. Some say it started with the agricultural revolution, others with the industrial revolution. And there are those who believe that the Anthropocene began with the emergence of humans. But whichever definition of the Anthropocene is the right one, they're all just tiny bits of time when looking at the planet's entire history.

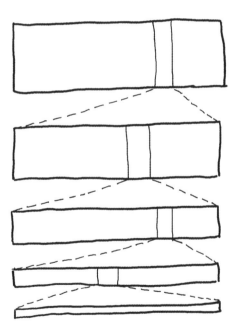

Fast Forward to Humanity

50,000 years ago, in the Late Palaeolithic era, various human species roamed the globe, including Homo sapiens, who had emerged approximately 250,000 years earlier. It's often suggested that different human species did not coexist, but evidence shows they did cross paths and even had children together. That's why Homo sapiens inherited various traits from other human species, that eventually ceased to exist.

Human intelligence

Three and a half million years ago, early humans discovered that meat was easier to digest than raw roots that required hard chewing. Initially, they were happy to eat predators' leftovers. Later, these primitive humans developed a hunting method — relentlessly chasing an animal until it overheated and collapsed. The next noteworthy development was the creation of stone tools for hunting, cutting meat, and grinding vegetables. Even with those tools, these early humans had to work hard to eat meat — a stark contrast to the industrial-scale meat farms of today.

Stacking Knowledge

The new diet led to changes in the human body: we got smaller teeth and jaw muscles. We also got larger brains and correspondingly bigger heads, which makes birth more challenging. That's why human babies are born 'prematurely' — as completely helpless beings who need care for a long time before they have any type of independence. During this period, however, children can learn a great deal (even more so because of those large brains).

Primatologist and psychologist Frans de Waal explains that humans are, first and foremost, just animals. What makes humans special is their ability to build upon existing knowledge — throughout generations. In essence, skyscrapers are evolved huts. This principle applies to all human inventions. Thomas Edison did not invent the lightbulb; he built on the inventions of many others to come up with a commercially successful version. The lightbulb was later used in the invention of the television, which led to the computer, and eventually, the smartphone. No idea is unique; every idea stems from another.[2]

> **Thinking isn't done by individuals;**
> **it is done by communities.** — Steven Sloman

Lost knowledge

British artist Thomas Thwaites set out to create a toaster from scratch, meaning he wanted to make every single part himself. For this, he needed iron. But Thwaites hit a snag because he could not find the information detailing the complete, step-by-step process for making iron in any contemporary sources. Due to innovation, that knowledge had been lost — nowadays, iron is produced exclusively in factories. Eventually, Thwaites discovered the process for making iron in a 15th-century book.

Of course, this was a very specific kind of project — but it's not unique for people to have lost what once was basic knowledge. Do you know how a Brussel sprout grows? Or how shoes are made? A hundred years ago, this was common knowledge. But the way our society has changed (in these cases, removed us from nature and craftsmanship), has made us forget. Luckily, a lot of knowledge has been put into books — and there's the Internet now.

2 → More about this in 'Don't Read This Book'

Unknown knowledge

Our ability to stack knowledge and generate ideas has long made us focus on ourselves when it comes to intelligence. Nowadays, we are learning more about other animal species — and their signature types of intelligence, abilities, and traits. And no matter how special we think we are, no human has the navigation skills of a shrimp, can camouflage like an octopus, or live as long as a Greenland shark.

Many animals experience Earth entirely differently than we do. They live differently, so they have a different perspective. Sometimes, this leads to misunderstanding. For a long time, human researchers thought that gibbons were a less intelligent type of ape compared to gorillas. However, it turned out that gibbons just experience the world differently: they live in trees and move mainly from top to bottom — vertically — while gorillas, like humans, live on the ground and move horizontally. Because gibbons (like gorillas) were judged from a human perspective and thus the human (horizontal) experience of life, they were mistakenly seen as less intelligent in comparison.

It's important to remember that our biases about what's 'normal' or 'smart' influence a lot of our judgments about animals — and about other people, too.

For decades now, we've been doing all these weird tests on animals to try and decide who gets to join the intelligence club. And they're all modelled on, of course, how humans do things.
— James Bridle

#2

IDEAS ARE STACKED KNOWLEDGE

No idea is truly unique. We're constantly inspired by things that already exist — created by humans, animals or plants. The strength of humans lies in our ability to collect knowledge and ideas. Reflect on what has been done, take what you can use, and pass it on.

How We Started Controlling Earth

Around 100,000 years ago, Homo sapiens began to migrate out of Africa, spreading across the world. They followed the wild game they could hunt. This migration was not continuous but occurred in phases when the climate was favourable. With the invention of the lockstitch (yes, the stitch that also keeps your jeans in one piece), people could sew hides together. This provided better protection against the cold, and thus more freedom to move into colder regions.

For a long time, it was believed that humans only started to influence nature with the emergence of extensive agriculture around 10,000 years ago. However, research by the University of Maryland, Baltimore County (UMBC) suggests that humans have impacted landscapes for much longer. In fact, according to the computer model they used, 10,000 years ago, only a quarter of Earth was what we would consider 'true' wilderness — humans had already left their mark. They might have led nomadic lifestyles and not have built cities yet, but these nomads did establish (temporary) settlements and used fire.

Land management by Neanderthals

Many archaeologists believe that around 12,000 years ago — with an estimated global population ranging from 2 to 10 million people — humans were already using fire to manage their immediate surroundings: for instance, to manipulate their environments into growing certain plants. A fascinating example of landscape management by Neanderthals was discovered in Germany. Archaeologists found evidence that around 125,000 years ago, the area near the Neumark-Nord site was influenced by its inhabitants. Oak forests had dominated the landscape until Neanderthals occupied and modified the region for a period of approximately 2,000 years. When the Neanderthals eventually left, the oak forests returned.

Agriculture = culture

We now know that agriculture emerged independently in about 10 different regions worldwide, and that the process was unique everywhere. Hunting, fishing, gathering, and agriculture formed a flexible mix of survival strategies for millennia. Early farmers were often lactose intolerant, but famine drove people to consume milk, which is why they became lactose tolerant. Obviously, agriculture faced challenges, but in the long run, it stabilized the food supply.

The prevailing belief is that as agricultural methods became more effective, people began to live in closer-knitted groups on smaller areas of land, leading to the development of permanent settlements, civilizations, political and cultural governance, and organized forms of religion. However, there are scientists who posit that complex human societies emerged long before the 'invention' of agriculture.

There is an important difference between the human societies of 10,000 years ago and our modern world: the global population has grown from max. 10 million to 8 billion(!) people. They all need food and shelter, and many would like much more than just the bare necessities — did you know that 80% of people has never been on an airplane? We were 'only' with 1 billion in the early 1800s, but according to projections, we could reach 10 billion by 2085 — followed by an equally rapid population decline.

WORLD POPULATION

World Population

8000	6000	4000
BCE	BCE	BCE

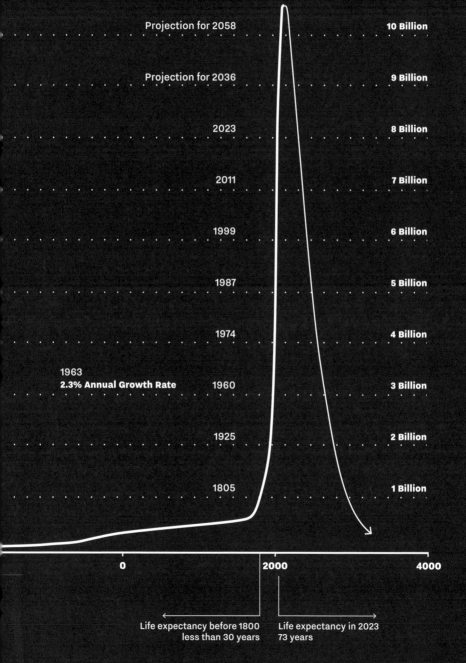

2100
-0.1% Annual Growth Rate

Projection for 2058   **10 Billion**

Projection for 2036   **9 Billion**

2023   **8 Billion**

2011   **7 Billion**

1999   **6 Billion**

1987   **5 Billion**

1974   **4 Billion**

1963
2.3% Annual Growth Rate   1960   **3 Billion**

1925   **2 Billion**

1805   **1 Billion**

0   2000   4000

Life expectancy before 1800   Life expectancy in 2023
less than 30 years   73 years

I've Got the Power

In medieval Western Europe, many people lived under a feudal system. The lucky few were born into a family of knights or nobles. The majority was born as a serf. Serfs lived and worked on the land owned by the lords, providing labour and resources. In exchange for their use of the land, the lords received a large portion of the produce, or other forms of payment. Serfs occupied the lowest rung on the societal ladder and had next to no rights. They served knights, who served nobles, who served a king. The knights and nobles agreed to serve in exchange for land and power. In return, the king expected their loyalty, their help managing the country and their willingness to raise an army against his enemies.

The power exchange

There has always been a link between people having needs and other people having or increasing their power by fulfilling those needs. You could even say that it's an exchange of commodities — although it often was, and still is, an unequal one. This exchange is the foundation of all forms of governance: the governed and government get something from each other.

> Elections have the undeniable advantage that everyone with the right to vote gets the opportunity to choose their representatives, but the downside is that participation is limited to designating others. The day on which you exercise your power is actually the day you give it away. — David Van Reybrouck

Greek economist Yanis Varoufakis said that religion and fear are important factors when it comes to power. If you can make people believe that you have the power to make the land fertile (something they need) because you know how to appease the higher power they believe in (and they're afraid of angering them), then you are well on your way to having a lot of influence and authority. That's why religion has always been an important tool to those seeking power and loyalty.

> **Religion was created by insecure men to oppress women. Religion is the basis of all political ideas and it exempts the human being to find the 'I' in them.** — Mutabaruka

When someone manages to gather people who are loyal, we can see the beginnings of a layered society. The specific form of governance does not really matter — whatever it is, it will usually result in a pyramid-like system where self-interest increases with height.

Let it go

There's a curious phenomenon that affects people at the top of the pyramid: the longer they hold power, the more challenging it becomes for them to hand it over. They become convinced that they are indispensable as leaders and will do whatever it takes to secure their position.

However, it doesn't have to be this way. Many (mainly male) leaders could learn something from the former Prime Minister of New Zealand, Jacinda Ardern. She served as Prime Minister from 2017 to 2023 and was praised for how she handled the country's economic and human aspects of the COVID-19 crisis. She is a leader that people from many other countries wished they had — someone you'd want to remain in leadership for a long while.

Ardern recognized when her energy was depleted (admitting when you can no longer do something is a strength) and handed over the reins. Providing direction is valuable, but passing on your power at the right time is a sign of true and selfless leadership.

The most common way people give up their power is by thinking they don't have any.
— Alice Walker

Hierarchies and self-organization

In the social sciences, there is significant debate about hierarchy. Some argue that hierarchy is a predominantly male construct. Frans de Waal suggests that there is an enormous number of mostly female hierarchies in the animal kingdom, and that hierarchies can be pretty useful.

Through self-organization, animals can create highly complex structures: beehives, termite cathedrals, beaver dams, weaver bird nests. Humans also achieve a lot through self-organization. When a building is constructed, it follows an architect's plans, but there is also a great deal of interaction among the construction workers. Similarly, in filmmaking, the director plays a creatively leading role, but a lot of work is done and decisions are made by other film industry professionals. Just look at the number of people on the end scroll (the credits). In cases like these, one could consider the work a 'gesamtkunstwerk' (total work of art).

According to De Waal, both animals and humans decide for themselves which group or project they want to join. In many cases, the initiator also becomes the de facto leader, but this doesn't mean that they will keep their position for ever. When leaders start to misbehave, they are removed from power, peacefully or violently so. History is full of leaders who were ultimately not tolerated.

Have you any idea how much tyrants fear the people they oppress? — Albus Dumbledore

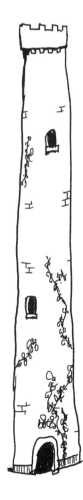

Money, Money, Money

According to anthropologist David Graeber (1961—2020), the state and the market emerged simultaneously and are interconnected, sort of like fraternal twins. Kings waged wars and needed soldiers, whom they had to pay. To acquire the money needed, they imposed taxes on the ordinary people, who, in turn, had to find ways to earn money. In summary, societies, including national economies, evolved into systems that provided rulers with soldiers and money. Because the possession of money became a need in society, profit and advantage became important concepts. Over time, the pursuit of material wealth became a central life goal.

Trading the World

The modern Western economy began in the 16th century when maritime trade started developing in Europe. New maritime routes gave a tremendous boost to world trade. The term 'world trade' might sound like fair trade across the seas, but in reality, it was largely about taking. English, Dutch, French, Spanish, and Portuguese ships were loaded with goods such as wool when they sailed to Asia. Once there, the merchandise was 'exchanged' for silk, spices, and other valuable goods which were then sold in Europe for a nice profit. Anyone who started trading in these new markets almost automatically became wealthy.

The feudal lords also noticed this trend. In England, many of them sent away the serfs from their land and replaced them with sheep because the wool was marketable internationally — the grains and vegetables grown by the serfs were not. After generations of having a meagre but relatively certain livelihood, many farm labourers suddenly lost it.

The feudal system ultimately stopped existing across Europe, sometimes due to the new international trade and sometimes due to a revolution, like in France. The result was the same: many former farm labourers moved to the city, where their only commodity was their labour — a product that could be purchased for wages. The former serfs might have been liberated from the feudal system, but they now worked in rich merchant families' factories — for nickels and dimes.

In the meantime, European trading nations had colonized large parts of the world. Until then, land had been one of the 3 essential factors of production (land, labour, and capital) and, thus, a factor of economic value. With the colonies added to the European homeland, land was abundant, and the concept of land scarcity no longer applied. The fact that other people already inhabited overseas land — or the idea that inhabited land should not be appropriated — didn't even cross the minds of Western Europeans. The resources supplied by the colonies seemed inexhaustible, including the labour of the indigenous people. They were seen as a very cheap or even free source of labour and more as property than as people.

Because of this development, the remaining economically relevant factors in Western Europe were labour and capital. The land was now considered part of the capital.

Slavery is not African history. Slavery interrupted African history.
— Mutabaruka

PRODUCTION FACTORS

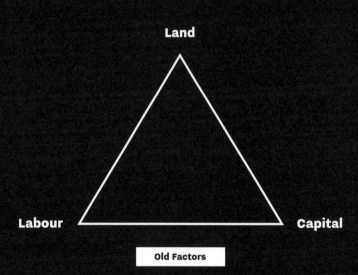

Land

Labour · · · · · · · · · · · · · · · · · · · Capital

Old Factors

Labour ———————————— Capital

New Factors

The 30 billion dollar debt

In the early 19th century, Haiti was France's most profitable colony. France operated the many plantations on the island with a staggering number of enslaved Africans.

After the Haitian Revolution, an agreement was reached in 1826 between Haiti and France. France would recognize Haiti's independence on the condition that Haiti pay 150 million francs as compensation for, among other things, the loss of land and the loss of enslaved Haitians. The first annual payment was 6 times Haiti's yearly income. By 1838, the payment had been reduced to 90 million francs, which, in today's terms, would be equivalent to over 30 billion dollars.

In 1888, Haiti made the final compensation payment to France. To make these payments, Haiti had to take out massive loans from a French bank, which primarily benefited the bank's shareholders. It would take until 1947 to fully repay the debt. Meanwhile, Haiti's economy had been completely shattered.

According to research by The New York Times, the extreme poverty the country is currently experiencing can be directly attributed to this debt. In 2016, the French government acknowledged that the compensation was unjust, but no money has been returned. And this is just one example of how colonization by Western European countries affects a country's current economy — there are many such cases. The Netherlands, where I am from, did a lot of damage in world history, too: as a keen participant in the transatlantic slave trade as well as a colonial oppressor.

There is no human failure greater than to launch a profoundly important endeavour and then leave it half done. This is what the West has done with its colonial system. It shook all the societies in the world loose from their old moorings. But it seems indifferent whether or not they reach safe harbour in the end.

— Barbara Ward

When the colonies were 'returned,' the cake was gone, and the indigenous inhabitants were left with nothing but crumbs. It's no wonder that many people today are still, to put it mildly, upset about the wealth that was built at the expense of their land and ancestors. They were stripped bare, and to this day, they continue to experience the consequences of the colonial era. Meanwhile, their oppressors' home countries have built exorbitantly rich economies with their stolen capital — and continue to exercise their (economic) power over the rest of the world.

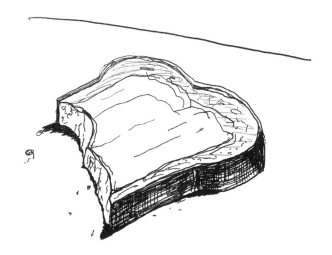

The Circular Flow

The ideas of John Maynard Keynes (1883—1964), the renowned British economist whose name appears in many people's school textbooks at least once, brought about fundamental changes in the economic policies of governments. After World War I, Keynes was a senior official. In that role, he attended the Versailles Peace Conference, but he resigned in protest before the treaty was signed. According to Keynes, the Versailles treaty did not prioritize the recovery of Europe; instead, it was a political act of revenge that would provoke a greater war (and he was right — see WWII).

In the 1970s, interest in Keynes' ideas waned, but since (or because of) the 2008 financial crisis, they have regained popularity. According to Keynes, an economy can spiral downward when households reduce their spending, as it causes businesses to produce less and consequently need fewer employees. This leads to more unemployment, and thus to even less spending by households. The government can counteract this negative spiral by increasing spending and financing projects that require more workers — reversing the downward spiral into an upward one.

Paul Samuelson visualized Keynes' ideas in his classic work 'Economics' (1948) as 'The Circular Flow': a closed, self-regulating system in which money circulates. At the centre of this model are businesses and households. Households provide labour and capital (production) in exchange for wages and profits. The households then spend this income on goods and services provided by businesses.

Money also exits this basic cycle and flows to banks, governments, and trade, which then reinject the money again. Banks convert household savings into investments; governments collect taxes and use them for public services; and then there are imports and exports.

THE CIRCULAR FLOW

Goods
& Services
Markets

Finished Products

Money

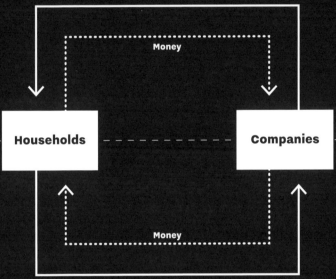

Households

Companies

Money

Labour, Capital, Land

Factor
Markets

The Circular Flow model had quite the impact on the science of economics. The model was used to make calculations about the flows in the system, but those calculations did not take reality into account — the social element was lost. Thus, economics, which started out as a social science, became a theoretical, mathematical science.

> **Too large a proportion of recent 'mathematical' economics are mere concoctions, as imprecise as the initial assumptions they rest on, which allow the author to lose sight of the complexities and interdependencies of the real world in a maze of pretentious and unhelpful symbols.** — John Keynes

The MONIAC

A year after the publication of 'Economics,' economist and engineer Bill Phillips constructed the first economic hydraulic computer model based on the Circular Flow: the MONIAC (Monetary National Income Analogue Computer), also known as the Financephalograph. Using pink fluid, the MONIAC demonstrates how money flows through the system.

It's a highly insightful model, but something is missing. This model may resemble a perpetual motion machine, but it's not. You see, to make something move, you need energy — which is why there were a plug and a switch on the MONIAC to turn it on.

Like the MONIAC demonstrates, we need energy to operate machines. We also need raw materials to make products, and food to sustain life. And just like the 'on' switch was hidden at the back of the MONIAC, we often don't see who or what provides the energy, and where the raw materials come from. Who it is that pays the price to keep the economy running?

How Banks Create Money

According to David Graeber, virtual currencies are not new at all; in fact, they are the origin of money. Credit systems, bills, and expense accounts are as old as civilization (and the barter system). Graeber also argued that debt and its forgiveness have played a crucial role in shaping the moral values of Western society. This is still observable in how banks are allowed to deal with other people's lives today.

Our modern monetary system is based on a virtual system built on debt. This system allows banks to create more and more money. Here's how it works: people (and businesses) deposit their money — their salaries and savings — in the bank. The bank holds on to this money. On your bank account, a number tells you how much money you have with the bank at the moment — how much money you could withdraw in theory. However, the bank also knows that almost everyone leaves their money in their bank account. They even pay you interest on the money you leave there, to make this more attractive. For the people who do want to withdraw their money, the bank only needs a minimal amount of cash — about 5% of the total money in people's accounts — because we don't all withdraw our money at the same time.

   The money the bank holds for you can be lent to someone else. When this happens, an amount is put into the borrower's account (for example, for a mortgage or investment), while the borrower now has a debt to the bank, on which they must pay interest. This is how the bank earns money.

As long as the bank keeps an eye on having about 5% in cash, it can lend much more money than it actually possesses. So, the bank lends out much more money than it actually holds. And because the borrower spends the borrowed money in our real world (at the bakery, at a construction company, etc.), the amount of money keeps growing.

This growth causes money to become less valuable (think about what you paid for a loaf of bread 10 years ago): inflation. Governments try to curb inflation via their central banks — by raising or lowering the interest rates on the loans that commercial banks take out.

Because banks profit from creating money, it's tempting for them to bet that not 5% of people will come to withdraw cash but only 2.5%. Some banks actually do this. And as long as everything goes according to plan and no more than 2.5% of the money is withdrawn, there's no problem…

But when it falls…

Until a bank gets into trouble. This can happen, for example, when asset managers can't repay their loans due to bad investments. In 2008, the asset management firm Lehman Brothers couldn't repay its debt. They had borrowed billions to invest in mortgages. When home prices suddenly plummeted, they went bankrupt and couldn't pay their debts to the banks. This led to the global credit crisis: banks went bankrupt, and their customers were also affected.

A bank run can occur when there is bad news about a bank and people then rush to the bank to withdraw their money. (Many physical banks were designed to be spacious enough so that a long queue couldn't form in front of the bank, avoiding the impression of a bank run.) During a bank run, the

bank cannot let every customer withdraw because they only have 5% cash or less. To get hold of lots of cash quickly, the
bank has to liquidate its outstanding investments. When this
doesn't generate enough cash and the bank collapses, the
bank's clients see their money vanish into thin air.

If the environment were a bank, it would have been saved by now.
— Bernie Sanders

That's where the government steps in. The government has
no interest in people having no money and rescues the bank
through capital injections or nationalization. So, when things
go wrong, the bankers are saved by the government, which uses taxpayers' money to protect its citizens. The result: bankers
become rich whether they muck up or not, while society
doesn't get anything in return. The bank always wins.

Shredding the system
In 2018, Banksy's 'Girl with Balloon,' a piece of graffiti art, was
auctioned off for $1.4 million. Banksy had built a paper shred-
der into the frame. When the hammer came down, and the
auction house guards tried to remove the painting, the artwork started to self-destruct. Due to a flaw in the mechanism,
the artwork was only partially shredded. Banksy renamed the
piece 'Love is in the Bin.' In 2021, it was sold again — this time
for $25.4 million. What was originally intended as a statement
against financial excesses in the art world ended up making an
already rich person another $24 million.

You're Scrooged

A popular television programme called Mindf*ck showed an interesting experiment involving the game of Monopoly. In every game, 1 of the 2 players received certain advantages: twice as much starting capital and a double amount of money when passing 'Go.' This player was also allowed to roll 2 dice. You can guess the outcome — but this experiment was not about who won. It was about the advantaged players' behaviour.

During the game, their behaviour became increasingly domineering, they visibly counted their money more often, became greedier, and refused to negotiate with the other players. The richer they became, the more nuts they took from the bowl that had been placed on the table — to share. At the end of the game, each advantaged player claimed that their tactics had led to their victory. None of them considered the fact that they had already started with a significant advantage. When people win, they tend to forget that many external factors help create the right circumstances for them to win. Remember Kim Kardashian's advice about how to be successful: "Get your fucking ass up and work. It seems like nobody wants to work these days."

Even if both players had started on an equal footing, it is still likely that one of them would have an advantage, possibly due to their background, the family they grew up in, or their line of work.

I must admit that I have played a lot of Monopoly. After a while, you become familiar with the tactics. I, too, would sit there counting my money like Scrooge McDuck. I remember one particular game when I was playing Monopoly with my friend, and his father started secretly taking money from the bank and giving it to him — capital injections. Since I was already winning, this money kept coming to me with each turn before he even had a chance to invest. I owned almost all the properties. I just kept getting richer while he couldn't make any progress.

MONEY MAKES MORE/LESS MONEY

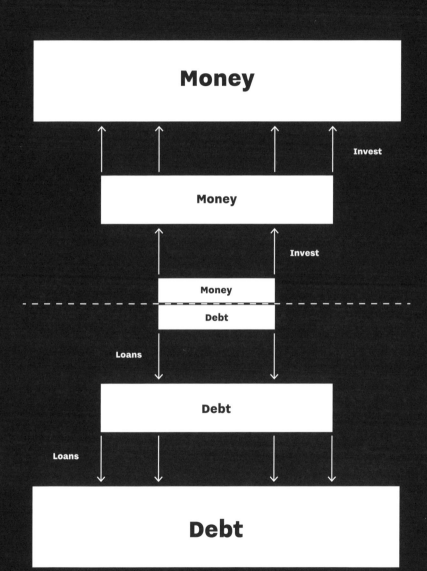

The Landlord's Game by Elizabeth Magie

Monopoly is often seen as the ultimate capitalist game, but this was not the game's original intention. In 1902, progressive Elizabeth Magie, a Scottish immigrant from Washington D.C., wanted to highlight the enormous income disparities and the power of monopolists. She created The Landlord's Game, in which players wouldn't follow a linear path (like in a game of Snakes and Ladders) but would move in circles. During those rounds, players would encounter all the things they come across in real life.

The game provided insight into how society works, highlighting the power of money and of cooperation. There were 2 sets of rules: an anti-monopolistic version where players cooperated, and a monopolistic version where each player tried to collect as much property and money as possible.

In 1903, she applied for a patent and released the game through the Economic Game Company, which she co-owned. For 30 years, The Landlord's Game was popular among left-wing intellectuals and students. Then, people from the Quaker community in Atlantic City discovered the game and created their own version using street names from their town. The game made the rounds in the community, and someone called Charles Darrow, who claimed that he invented it, eventually took the game to Parker Brothers. Parker Brothers released it as Monopoly, with only the monopolistic rules we know now. To secure their monopoly on Monopoly, they bought all the rights from Magie for $500.

The Parker Brothers and Charles Darrow became incredibly wealthy from the royalties. The world had forgotten The Landlord's Game and Elizabeth Magie until 1973, when economics professor Ralph Anspach released an anti-monopoly version aptly called Anti-Monopoly. When he was sued by the Parker Brothers, Anspach uncovered Magie's original patent — and won the case.

If a monkey hoarded more bananas than it could eat, while most of the other monkeys starved, scientists would study that monkey to figure out what the heck was wrong with it. When humans do it, we put them on the cover of Forbes.

— Nathalie Robin Justice Gravel

#3

NOTHING COMES FROM NOTHING

You cannot create something out of nothing. In the end, someone or something always pays the price. Consider, when you create something: what are the resources, where do they come from? Who gets to profit, and who ends up paying the price?

TO THE
PRESENT
THE
STAKEHOLDERS

Resistance does not begin with big words, but with small deeds.

— Remco Campert

The Rise of the Consumer

We live in a house, wear clothes, and eat food and to be able to do so, we work. Initially, we worked to be self-sufficient; later, to buy products. Until the beginning of the Industrial Revolution, most of us consumed what we needed. After that, as Erich Fromm said in his book 'Socialist Humanism,' we became the 'Homo Consumens'.

> I mean the bare necessities,
> old mother nature's recipes, that bring
> the bare necessities of life. — Baloo

At the time of the Industrial Revolution, people moved to the cities to work in the factories. The working conditions there were hellish. When workers started to unite in trade unions, their situation improved gradually. Because workers need their jobs, but employers also need workers. They are dependent on each other. By organizing strikes, workers could demand better conditions. Working hours became shorter, wages rose, work became safer bit by bit, and people got time to enjoy life a little.

Production for Profit

Around 1900, manufacturers increasingly used assembly lines to enable mass production. Especially in the USA, the number of shops grew rapidly, and huge department stores with multiple floors made their debut. The focus shifted from need-to-haves to want-to-haves. The department stores had only one goal: selling as many items as possible. It was production-for-profit, with temptation as the primary means of selling. Welcome to the consumer economy.

In a consumer society, people wallow in things, fascinating, enjoyable things. If you define your value by the things you acquire and surround yourself with, being excluded is humiliating.

— Zygmunt Bauman

Entrepreneurs, economists, and politicians unanimously agreed that stimulating consumption was essential to maintain economic growth. Producers should not wait for demand; they had to create it. Creative directors, marketeers, designers and copywriters enticed people to stop making their own clothes and to start buying ready-made luxury fashion. The prevailing belief was that buying products would raise your standard of living and make you happier.

This new idea that an endless need for new products and services could be created, was seen as the height of economic progress. The Holy Grail of inexhaustible fortune and wealth had been discovered.

Electricity is key

In 1929, almost 7 in 10 of American homes had electricity. This widespread availability of electricity enabled the sale of various other electrical appliances. Only some people had the money to buy these things, but the rest could buy on instalment (paying in small portions, plus interest). Soon, many households owned refrigerators, vacuum cleaners, and radios.

With the arrival of commercial radio, products could suddenly be promoted in people's private space — in their homes. That promotion platform only became bigger with the introduction of television. If people wanted to listen to music or watch a programme, they would also encounter commercials for the next luxury product. An endless stream of merchandise, marketed in commercials as freedom and, on a meta-level, as prestige and happiness, flooded into consumers' homes. Here, we see the modern market and society in action: what starts as a luxury for the happy few later becomes standard for everyone, which creates further demand for even more extreme luxury. This seems to have become a never-ending cycle.

> **What you call love was invented by guys like me... to sell nylons.** — Don Draper

Harder, better, faster, stronger

Manufacturers wanted to ensure that people would continue buying. Some say that they used a new strategy to accomplish this: 'planned obsolescence' — the intentional manufacture of products that would need replacement quickly. In practice, production often seems to be driven by other motivations — there's little to no thought given to quality or lifespan. For manufacturers, the more pressing question is: how do I put a product on the market as quickly and cheaply as possible?

So, paradoxically, a so-called high standard of living was created with inferior products: lots of them, that had to be replaced fast. There would always be something bigger or better to sell — to a 'free' market that was always hungry. What more could a capitalist want?

Send it to me before I want it.
— Ronny Chieng

Humpty Dumpty and the Invention of the Shopping Cart

Sylvan Goldman, owner of the Humpty Dumpty supermarket chain in Oklahoma City, made an observation about his customers: when their shopping baskets became too heavy, they headed to the checkout rather than continue shopping. In 1937, Goldman had a eureka moment. Together with his maintenance man, he built a prototype: a steel frame with two shopping baskets stacked on top of each other, with wheels underneath — the first shopping cart.

Goldman hired models to showcase the cart. They spent the day walking through the stores, putting items in their shopping carts — and it worked. The shopping cart became a success. Monkey see, monkey do.

In 1946, Orla Watson from Kansas City came up with an updated version. He invented a way to nest the carts into each other, saving store space. Then, Goldman made the carts bigger so that they could hold even more items. This cart model is still used in today's supermarkets — and shopping websites, in the top right corner. Click 'Add to Cart.'

The products you add to your shopping cart need to be shipped to the store first — often from far away. Another seemingly simple invention plays a significant role in this process. It is a steel box that became the backbone of the consumer society. Thanks to this box, we can eat Peruvian blueberries in Europe; we can buy questionably cheap clothing; and stuff our homes with electronics. Most of the stuff we have has at some point been inside such a box: the container.

How the Container Moved the World

Malcom McLean was a self-made man — his story is a classic example of the 'American Dream.' As a student, he worked at a gas station. By 1935, he had saved enough to buy a second-hand truck for $120. He founded the McLean Trucking Co. with his sister Clara and brother Jim.

McLean was a driver himself and often delivered goods to ports. There, he saw that each crate was hoisted into the hold separately — it was a time-consuming and labour-intensive process. The railways had experimented with lifting entire trailers with cargo onto ships, but this took up too much space. What if you only lifted the trailer box into the hold?

When McLean sold the trucking business for $25 million in 1955, he bought the Pan-Atlantic Steamship Company. He used his trucking expertise in his new business and converted the ship SS Ideal X[1] into a container ship. A year later, the SS Ideal X sailed a distance of 2,500 kilometres with 58 containers on board.

1 → The SS Ideal X was the world's second container ship.
The first container ship was the Clifford J. Roger.

At this time, the cost of transporting a ton of cargo had been $5.86. With McLean's containers, it dropped to just 16 cents. Despite this price difference, interest in his shipping services was initially limited for several reasons: many ports lacked the cranes needed for loading and unloading, and dock workers' unions feared for job security.

It was the USA military who made the first important step into popularising the use of shipping containers. The military had experimented with containers before but used them at a grand scale for the first time during the Vietnam War. This was the beginning of a growing global demand for shipping containers.

Big, bigger, biggest

McLean released several essential patents royalty-free to the International Organization for Standardization (ISO) to stimulate industry growth. Within a few years, a global standard size for containers was established, and infrastructure worldwide was adapted: the length and width of ships, trains, trucks, tracks, roads, ports, cranes, viaducts, and information systems. "The container has been a bigger driver of globalization than all trade agreements of the past 50 years combined," wrote The Economist.

The cost of global transport dropped to less than 1% of a product's selling price. That's why it became highly profitable for companies to manufacture their products in low-wage countries and then ship them to wealthy countries. Of course, this production method was not new; it had a long colonial history. For centuries, valuable resources and cheap labour or slavery in (former) colonies were used to produce goods that the locals could not afford. These countries, colonies or not, were all exploited with a colonial mindset. Their resources were used for products that were then shipped to the industrialized world. That's where the money was.

These days, the largest container ships transport more than 24,000 containers per vessel. However, these mega-ships require massive investments. And as it happens in a free market, the big companies outcompeted the small ones, leading to shipping companies either merging or going bankrupt. As a result, 10 shipping companies[2] with a total fleet of more than 3500 ships (and counting) dominate the current global container shipping industry. These shipping companies collaborate in 3 alliances that determine the rules of the global economy. Combined, these companies generate profits of more than $200 billion — roughly the GDP of a country like Qatar.

When morality comes up against profit, it is seldom that profit loses. — Shirley Chisholm

What's not included...

The shipping companies also determine which ports participate in their worldwide shipping network. If a port is part of the network, it must ensure that the enormous ships can dock and be unloaded quickly. For example, the port of Rotterdam handles around 15 million containers annually. That's 30 containers per minute!

Concentrating all these ships in just a few places leads to significant air pollution in those areas. The emissions of CO_2 and other pollutants, and the costs for the ports to accommodate these ships, are not paid for by the shipping companies. They are paid for by the taxpayer. Companies in Europe or the OECD normally pay between 25% and 30% corporate tax, but shipping companies pay only 0.5% to 2% tax. They are not taxed on their profits but on the volume of their ships. It's so convenient, they don't even have to try to evade any taxes.

2 → MSC, APM-Maersk, CMA CGM, COSCO, Hapag-Lloyd, ONE, Evergreen, HMM, Yang Ming, Wan Hai.

...But what is included

Because of the way they're (barely) taxed, the shipping companies' services can remain cheap: they don't need to raise the prices of products to offset any cost of taxes or emissions. And then there's another issue: air is one of the most shipped products. This is because many goods get shipped from Asia to Europe and the USA, but not vice versa — which means that about ⅓ of all containers are empty when transported back to Asia. Those emissions are made for literally nothing.

The good news is that there are efforts underway to develop collapsible containers. Of course, even the most efficient collapsible container will not solve every issue caused by global shipping. For instance, unwanted invasive species often hitch a ride to the other side of the world where they happily threaten or even demolish local ecosystems that contain none of their natural enemies.

353,264 Daisies

All kinds of products are transported all over the world in shipping containers. Sometimes, that has unforeseen consequences. In 1997, a ship called Tokyo Express lost 62 containers near the coast of Cornwall, England. One of these containers held 4.8 million Lego pieces. To this day, Lego figures and bricks wash up on the shores of Cornwall. Many of the Lego pieces have a maritime theme — like black octopuses or flippers — making them particularly popular. Dragons have been found, too, as well as 353,264 Lego daisies. Some enterprising local children search for rare Lego pieces on the beach and sell them to tourists.

Although the pieces have officially only been reported along the coast of Cornwall, they could have travelled more than 62,000 miles — and wash up on any beach in the world, for many years to come.

Oil kindles extraordinary emotions and hopes, since oil is above all a great temptation. It is the temptation of ease, wealth, strength, fortune, power. It is a filthy, foul-smelling liquid that squirts obligingly up into the air and falls back to Earth as a rustling shower of money.

— Ryszard Kapuściński

In Black Gold We Trust

Did you know that Lego bricks are made with oil? Oil has been at the foundation of nearly every aspect of our consumer society. In 1859, the first drilling rig was installed. Just a few years earlier, it had been discovered how to make lamp oil from crude oil, which caused the demand for oil to surge. When surface oil supplies were quickly depleted, deeper drilling became necessary. These drilling rigs made fortunes for a few people and provided work for the ordinary folk.

Oil powers our cars, propels our ships, and heats our homes. It's also the raw material for countless items in our everyday lives, from plastic containers and bags in the supermarket to computers, toys, and medical instruments. Modern life depends on oil.

Today's society is so much dependent on oil, that the economic confidence index is measured by the price of crude oil. When an oil producing country announces changes in its oil production, this immediately affects the stock markets. And the stronger the recovery of oil prices after a dip, the more traveling, driving, flying, and producing is done. That's why oil producers have an enormous amount of power — so much power that politics can't control it.

The growing demand for oil

Despite the fact that oil has been pumped for about 150 years, 83% of the world has only just started consuming it, according to Forbes business magazine. Rich countries, which comprise only 17% of the world's population, use 50% of the world's available oil.

Poor countries are not 'underdeveloped', they are over-exploited.
— Michael Parenti

Of course, it is precisely the oil-dependent Western countries that cannot stop talking about the transition to green energy. That's all nice and easy when you have already profited from oil and the prosperity that comes with it — while that oil often comes from countries where the inhabitants mainly bear the burden of the oil industry but see nothing in return (except corruption, pollution, and health problems - I'm looking at you, Shell, ExxonMobil, Chevron, BP...).

17% of the people cannot dictate that the other 83% should not profit from the oil industry. That smells like green colonialism. The only way forward is to ensure that this 83% gets access to the same level of prosperity, but that we find ways to do this without the use of oil and with the use of renewable energy. And, of course, the wealthy West needs to go green itself rather than telling the rest of the world what to do.

> **To be good is noble. To tell people how to be
> good is even nobler and much less trouble.**
> — Mark Twain

The humble servants of society

Back in the 1970s, in-house researchers at ExxonMobil already
had a detailed forecast for what would happen at current
fossil fuel consumption rates. This forecast predicted global warming remarkably accurately. ExxonMobil chose to do
nothing with this information — quite the opposite: they publicly denied any link between oil and global warming. Making
money from the ever-increasing demand for fossil energy was
more important than what it would do to the planet. And it
still is, apparently...

Former Shell CEO Ben van Beurden wrote on LinkedIn "Imagine Shell decided to stop selling petrol and diesel today. This
would certainly cut Shell's carbon emissions. But it would not
help the world one bit. Demand for fuel would not change.
People will fill up their cars and delivery trucks at other service stations."

This kind of excuse — "If I don't do it, someone else will"
— is an easy cop-out. You would think that someone of Van
Beurden's stature has the phone numbers of all other fossil
industry big shots. In other words: if people like him really
wanted to take responsibility, they could.

Corporations like to present themselves as serving the
greater good. They claim to foster innovation and increase
wealth, which helps societies grow and develop. As 'servants
of society,' the government grants them certain freedoms and
privileges in return. This is not a recent phenomenon. It ex-
isted way before the industrial revolution — even in the Roman Empire, there was a type of company called the societas
publicanorum (which had shareholders and was limited in
liability).

The bigger the companies become, the more dependent society becomes on the jobs and products they provide. Companies need society as a workforce and as their market. But ultimately — and this is very evident today — society becomes the servant of the corporations. The corporations' executives are given excessive bonuses and shareholders receive the profits while the workers' wages lag behind, or don't even get a liveable wage. We all know how Walmart staff was grossly underpaid and had to rely on government aid to survive; we've all heard about the work conditions and unbearable pressure at Amazon. Only after immense criticism (and most likely, fear of more PR nightmares) did these companies try to change something in their policies. And even then, it's not enough. They don't really care about their people.

Most companies do not spontaneously invest money in their employees' well-being or the preservation of the Earth. To make this happen, we need more than corporations: we need governments willing to enforce employee rights and Earth rights.

REGULATION SYSTEM

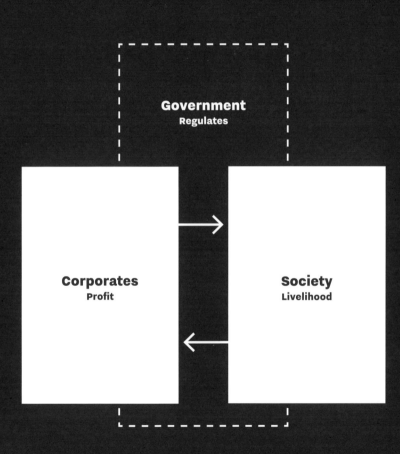

#4

BE AWARE OF THE SIDE EFFECTS

We continuously invent things that make life easier and more efficient. Be aware that what you create may have significant consequences — positive and negative. Consider all possible developments.

200.000 Plastic Bottles per Minute

In 2019, The Coca-Cola Company announced that they produce 3 million tons of plastic packaging for all their soft drink and water brands annually. That's 200,000 bottles per minute. In the 1950s, Coca-Cola still used a refill system: empty glass bottles were cleaned and refilled. With the introduction of plastic bottles, they were able to move away from the refill system. It was up to society to introduce deposit systems. But that was not a priority at a time when — exactly because of the invention of plastic — the height of luxury was to have single use items. No washing or carrying, just throw it away after use!

There is no such thing as 'away'. When we throw anything away, it must go somewhere.

— Annie Leonard

Recyclable or recycled?

Nowadays, Coca-Cola has various sustainability plans, but these have a lot of fine print. Similar companies like Nestle and PepsiCo also claim to have plans but don't disclose any figures. Plus, such plans often have gaps in them: for example, their recycling programs depend on deposit systems, which do not exist in every country. This means that even though plastic is recyclable in theory, it is often not recycled in practice.

There are other difficulties with recycling plastic: it cannot be recycled when it is a mix of different types. And it shows: of the 9 billion tons of plastic produced so far, a disappointing 9% was recycled, and only 1% was recycled multiple times. The rest ends up in landfills — often in low and middle-income countries, where it is exported to. Or it ends up as microplastics in the plastic soup, our groundwater, and thus in our food — it even ends up in breast milk.

In the circular economy concept, waste is a resource. It changes the production model from 'take → make → waste' to 'make → waste → make'. Recycling does come with some notes, though: firstly, you need new energy to turn waste into a new raw material. Secondly, you have to add extra raw material to the recycled material — because the more often it is recycled, the weaker it becomes. Another point of attention is the fact that sometimes, we transfer raw material to another chain in the process or recycling. For instance, it's excellent that clothing is made from PET bottles, but that also means new PET bottles are going to be produced.

Waste is a design flaw.
— Kate Krebs

Plastic filled with water

Worldwide, more than 1 million bottles of water are sold every minute. For the USA alone, it takes 17 million barrels of oil per year to produce enough plastic water bottles. Meanwhile, clean drinking water is also readily available from the tap in many places. There, people are paying for the bottle: for the luxury of twisting a cap instead of turning a faucet.

Is it better to sell water and soft drinks in glass or aluminium? Not necessarily: aluminium requires mining and glass is heavier to transport. If fewer soft drinks were consumed, we would need less packaging. And it would help our health too, because soft drinks may taste good, but they are not good for you. The World Obesity Federation estimates that by 2035, half of the world's population will be overweight or obese, costing 4 trillion dollars per year in healthcare. Is this all because the customer really wants to consume unhealthy products? Or is it because the companies want the customer to want them? What is the symptom, and what is the disease?

> **The most threatening act of protest for a capitalist system would be for its citizens to refuse to consume.**
> — Fiona Raby and Anthony Dunne

Fast Fashion on Steroids

It's not just plastic that is being discarded. Every year, 92 million tons of textile waste are produced. This is not surprising when you consider that between 80 and 100 billion new garments are made each year.

According to a UN report from 2019, global clothing production doubled between 2000 and 2004. The report also states that the clothing industry is "responsible for 20% of total water waste on a global level". We don't need all those clothes. According to the British Fashion Council, there is enough clothing in the world to dress all people for the next 6 generations.

Clothing is often produced in Asian countries like Bangladesh, India or China, then travels through Europe and the USA and eventually ends up in places like the Atacama Desert in Chile. Every year, 59,000 tons of clothing arrive in the port of Iquique, where some of it is resold. But most of it, at least 39,000 tons, is dumped in the desert. Google 'Atacama clothes' to see some really shocking pictures. It's no wonder that the UN calls it "an environmental and social emergency".

Over the last decade, public awareness about fast fashion has grown substantially. However, a lot of brands just use it as a marketing ploy: for instance, they say that their items are sewn to order (while this is hardly ever the case in fast fashion).

Initiatives have been set in motion on political levels, too. The EU has been working to get textile industry policies in place, most importantly a ban on the destruction of unsold clothing. The EU also aims "to make producers responsible for the full lifecycle of textile products and to support the sustainable management of textile waste across the EU."

Buy less, choose well, make it last
— Vivienne Westwood

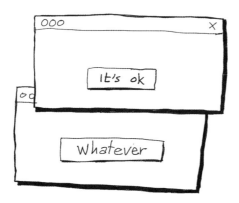

No Such Thing as a Free Lunch

For a long time, if you ordered a beer at a saloon, you would also get a 'free' lunch. This lunch was loaded with salt, so you would drink more. In the end, you always paid for your lunch, even if you didn't realize it.

Capitalism is not just a system but also a mentality: a continuous dissatisfaction and craving for more. More things, more experiences, more travel, more earnings. It's a drive for boundless growth that exhausts everything. People, animals, and the Earth. One way or another, we will pay for the free lunch.

> **People are flying into Las Vegas airport in order to get to Death Valley in the hope of being there when a new all-time highest temperature record is set.** — James Dyke

'The Limits of Growth' and the Club of Rome

In 1968, a group of people, later known as the Club of Rome, met at Villa Farnesina in Rome. The group consisted of scientists, diplomats, businesspeople, and others. The meeting was initiated by Italian industrialist Aurelio Pecci and British scientist Alexander King, who felt that global problems needed to be effectively addressed.

Their goal was to investigate the interconnections of global problems and to alert the world to their seriousness. They created a computer simulation to examine the effects of economic and population growth, while taking into consideration that natural resources are finite. Factors such as food production, industrialization, population growth, the depletion of natural resources, and pollution were entered into the computer with various parameters — revolutionary at the time. The conclusion was that if consumption patterns did not change, both the population and the industrial capacity would decline suddenly and uncontrollably.

The findings were published in 1972 under the title 'The Limits of Growth.' Partly due to the oil crisis a year later, 'The Limits of Growth' became a bestseller, with 30 million copies sold in over 30 languages. The message that the world was moving towards self-destructive overconsumption was not entirely new. Other books with ominous titles like 'Famine 1975!' had been published in the decade before, predicting disasters and the end of abundance.

1.75 Earths

International think tank Global Footprint Network calculates Earth Overshoot Day each year: "the date when humanity has used all the biological resources that Earth regenerates during the entire year."

In 1970, Earth Overshoot Day fell at the end of December. Back then, 1 Earth was enough. 50 years later, this day falls at the end of July or the beginning of August. This means that globally, we need 1.75 Earths on average to keep the entire economic machine running.

If the entire world population used resources at the same rate as Uruguayans, we would need only 0.7 Earths. However, the lifestyle of European countries consumes many times more: 3 to 4.5 Earths. The USA is at 5 Earths. And if the whole world lived like Qatar, 8.9 Earths would be needed each year. The fact that we 'use' 1.75 Earths per year, and that we only have 1.0 Earth, naturally has consequences.

IPCC Reports

The IPCC (Intergovernmental Panel on Climate Change) was established in 1988 by the UN to assess and promote scientific knowledge about climate change. It has 195 member states and allows scientists and governments to collaborate. Together, they evaluate research published in scientific journals and they release a report every 5 to 6 years.

One of the most recent reports (from March 2023) states: "Human activities, principally through emissions of greenhouse gases, have unequivocally caused global warming, with global surface temperature reaching 1.1°C above 1850—1900 in 2011—2020. Global greenhouse gas emissions have continued to increase, with unequal historical and ongoing contributions arising from unsustainable energy use, land use and land-use change, lifestyles, and patterns of consumption and production."

The report also describes the consequences of those changes: "Widespread and rapid changes in the atmosphere, ocean, cryosphere, and biosphere have occurred. Human-caused climate change is already affecting many weather and climate extremes in every region across the globe. This has led to widespread adverse impacts and related losses and damages to nature and people (high confidence). Vulnerable communities historically contributing the least to climate change are disproportionately affected."

If humanity massively invests in sustainability, the temperature increase by the end of this century will be 1.6°C. If we continue to use fossil fuels at the current rate, it will be 4.4°C. Whichever it will be, increased extreme weather conditions are a certainty — from extreme drought to heavy rainfalls. A century ago, a heatwave occurred once every 50 years. At a temperature rise of 1.6 degrees, it will be 8 times as frequent. At a rise of 4.4 degrees, it will be 39(!) times as frequent.

Besides the devastating effect on nature and biodiversity, these weather extremes will cause economic problems. Low-income countries are the most sensitive — exactly where the products the West is addicted to are made. But extreme heat and heavy rainfalls can also disrupt the economy in wealthier countries, causing enormous financial damage. In the long term, doing nothing about climate change is more expensive.

OK, but where is the apocalypse?

Critics of the IPCC reports say that the scientists work with outdated models and data. They also take issue with the methodology of World Overshoot Day. World Overshoot Day may be fantastic for awareness, but you cannot base policy on it.

And what about the Club of Rome's doomsday scenario — has that come true? Our lives have only gotten better. No disasters, but we do buy the latest fashion, go on faraway vacations, and drive expensive cars... or is that precisely the problem?

Many scientists say that the most disastrous effects of global warming are not visible now but will be in a few decades. They argue that measures must be taken to prevent worse outcomes. Other parties say: we can all see that nothing has happened, and therefore, climate change is a hoax.

We pretend we can solve this through market mechanisms. But 'green capitalism' is a myth, a way to play the system once again.

— Katharina Pistor

In 2007, 'An Inconvenient Truth', which featured Al Gore, received an Oscar for Best Documentary. The documentary and Gore also received criticism, and not only from climate deniers. Some scientists felt that Gore's documentary was getting in the way of the climate conversation and that they constantly had to explain what was really happening.

The documentary, as well as the books and reports were, in any case, a wake-up call. They led, among other things, to the Paris Agreement, a treaty with the main goal of cutting the emission of greenhouse gases next to other measures to tackle climate change. This agreement involved countries, but also so-called non-state actors like businesses, financial institutions, citizens, and local governments. The Paris Agreement has definitely had an effect, but it has not created serious enough climate policy — with firm agreements that structurally change something.

We are trotting slowly behind a climate that is changing at a gallop.

— Valérie Masson-Delmotte

The Possibility of Behaviour Change

In 2012, rockstar economist Kate Raworth introduced a ground-breaking economic model: the doughnut, which became the foundation of her book 'Doughnut Economics'. The model was immediately embraced by climate scientists and environmental movements.

Simply put, the goal of Doughnut Economics is to meet the needs of everyone within the Earth's carrying capacity. In her model, Raworth combines the UN's Sustainable Development Goals (SDGs), such as 'no hunger' and 'clean water and sanitation' with the 9 ecological ceilings as described by a group of Earth scientists for example, 'biodiversity loss' and 'climate change.'[3]

The doughnut's inner part represents humanity's basic needs (the UN's SDGs). The outer circle of the doughnut indicates the ecological limits of the Earth. "A safe and just space for humanity" lies between the two circles. The idea is that no one falls into the hole of the doughnut, and at the same time, we do not exceed the Earth's ecological limits and fall off the doughnut.

3 → The 17 Sustainable Development goals are here: https://sdgs.un.org/goals. The 9 ecological ceilings are: climate change, ocean acidification, chemical pollution, nitrogen, and phosphorus loading (overuse of fertilizer), freshwater withdrawals, land conversion, biodiversity loss, air pollution and ozone layer depletion.

How do we achieve this? New rules for all types of industry will help, but we also need to look at people's behaviour. Can it change?

> **You cannot get through a single day without having an impact on the world around you. What you do makes a difference, and you have to decide what kind of a difference you want to make.** — Jane Goodall

Nudge me a little

People are not necessarily inherently selfish. That was the outcome of research by the English division of the World Wildlife Fund (WWF) on the willingness of the British to adjust their lifestyle for the sake of the Earth's liveability. The survey asked about topics such as reducing meat and dairy consumption, imposing a maximum speed on highways, and implementing a progressive tax on flying. A remarkable 77% to 94% of people questioned turned out to be in favour of these adjustments, and they were willing to go much further than government policy. They also felt that they could use some nudging from the government.

> **A nudge, as we will use the term, is any aspect of the choice architecture that alters people's behaviour in a predictable way without forbidding any options or significantly changing their economic incentives.**
> — Richard H. Thaler and Cass Sunstein

According to the IPCC, behavioural change could reduce global emissions by 40% to 70% by 2050. That means that a large impact could be made through making different consumer choices, for instance about food or transportation. However, people do need to be 'nudged' into choosing these the alternative options by making them attractive, practical, and affordable — something creative people (like us!) can no doubt help with. To make this possible, we need to take a good hard look at how elements of society like transportation and food are currently organized. Then, we'll be able to see what we can change at a systemic level.

Let's Take Cars for Example...

In 1886, Carl Benz received patent DRP 37435 'Vehicle with gas engine operation' for a three-wheeled vehicle powered by a gas engine. Around that time, many inventions were being made — and patents applied for — that collectively resulted in the automobile. Benz was not the only person to create an automobile, or even the first one. A man called Siegfried Marcus had come up with a similar car at least 15 years before Benz did — but the nazis erased him from public memory because he was Jewish.

In the USA, cars were a hit from the start (in Europe, it would take until after WWII). In 1908, Henry Ford introduced the Ford Model T. With the help of the assembly line, a Model T could be assembled in 93 minutes. By 1927, there were 15 million of them in the world.

Ford and others were also working on electric cars at that time, but fossil fuel cars were easier to produce and had a much bigger radius. Compared to horse-drawn trams and carriages, with their wooden wheels and the horses' horseshoes, the car was extremely quiet.

Rubber from Congo

Due to the enormous demand for cars, there was a great need for tires, and thus for rubber. Belgian King Leopold II saw an opportunity to set up a rubber trade from colonized Congo. At the time, Congo was Leopold's private property, and he maintained a horrific pace in rubber production. In many cases, villagers were given daily quota for the rubber they needed to deliver. When they failed, the consequences were gruesome.

There is a famous photo, taken in 1904, of a Congolese man called Nsala, staring at what's left of his family: his 5-year-old daughter's hand and foot. The woman who took the photograph was missionary and photographer Alice Seeley Harris:

"He hadn't made his rubber quota for the day so the Belgian-appointed overseers had cut off his daughter's hand and foot. Her name was Boali. She was five years old. Then they killed her. But they weren't finished. Then they killed his wife too. And because that didn't seem quite cruel enough, quite strong enough to make their case, they cannibalized both Boali and her mother. And they presented Nsala with the tokens, the leftovers from the once living body of his darling child whom he so loved. His life was destroyed. They had partially destroyed it anyway by forcing his servitude but this act finished it for him. All of this filth had occurred because one man, one man who lived thousands of miles across the sea, one man who couldn't get rich enough, had decreed that this land was his and that these people should serve his own greed.

Leopold had not given any thought to the idea that these African children, these men, and women, were our fully human brothers, created equally by the same Hand that had created his own lineage of European Royalty."[4]

The colonial reign of terror, according to the most recent estimates, cost the lives of 10 million Congolese.

Thanks to all the produced rubber, people in the West could comfortably drive their cars. For them, the car became the ultimate symbol of freedom. It allowed people to live in leafy suburbs. It meant that shopping could be done once a week, leaving time for hobbies. The car had practical and cultural consequences all over the world. But clearly, the consequences were far from the same everywhere.

Clueless hicks

Until 1920, the streets in the USA were public spaces. People walked wherever they wanted. When cars started driving on the roads, there were many accidents involving pedestrians. Motorists were not very popular, and they were often convicted of manslaughter in cases of fatal accidents.

In 1923, 42,000 residents of Cincinnati submitted a peti-

4 → This is Seeley Harris' account from 'Don't Call Me Lady: The Journey of Lady Alice Seeley Harris' by Judy Pollard Smith.

tion to enact a law that limited the speed of cars to 25 miles per hour. Car manufacturers, auto dealers, and drivers came up with a different proposal: pedestrians should no longer be allowed to walk freely on the streets. This would prevent them from being hit by cars. It is clear which proposal prevailed.

The auto industry worked on its PR in many ways. For instance, it was happy to lend a hand by setting up a 'wire service.' Journalists could send a few details to The National Automobile Chamber of Commerce in case of an accident. They would then receive a ready-made article in return — in which the pedestrian was always the one to blame.

Safety campaigns were organized in schools. These 'campaigns' would now be called 'public shaming events'. For example, in 1925, a 12-year-old student who had crossed the street unsafely was subjected to a 'student trial' and sentenced to a week of cleaning blackboards.

The best-known campaign involved clowns pretending to cross the street unsafely — repeatedly 'colliding' with a slowly driving car. This is how the term jaywalking came into existence: 'Jay' was slang for 'clueless hick'. It later became an official term and an offense that could result in a fine. The street had finally become a public space exclusively for car owners.

Safety for the happy few

The streets haven't become much safer. After WWII, the construction of (high)ways exploded. The idea was that traffic must flow because time is money, so saving time is good for prosperity. Cities began to organize their entire infrastructures to facilitate people driving cars. This has had all sorts of consequences.

To make way for larger roads, blocks of houses were demolished. These were primarily the homes of low-income and minority communities. This phenomenon was so widespread that there was even a saying for it in the USA: "White men's roads through Black men's homes." The relatively poor communities the roads were built through usually didn't benefit

DEADLY ACCIDENTS

In the USA, 2020

42,915

3

People
Killed by
Cars

People
Killed by
Sharks

much from the new highways. In addition, safety measures for pedestrians were minimal in these neighbourhoods. And then there were the harmful exhaust fumes and fine particles — an added health risk with long-term effects.

The relatively high risk for people of colour to be hit by a car seems to have remained unchanged since the construction of those first roads. Smart Growth America, an organization that empowers communities to create liveable places, reported that "From 2010 to 2019, Black pedestrians were 82% more likely to be hit by a driver than white pedestrians."

In the USA alone, in 2020, 42,915 people died in car accidents. That same year, 3 people in the USA died from shark attacks. How much did you hear in the media about those shark attacks? And how much did you hear about the car accidents? Exactly. There's a lot of fuss about those 3 shark attacks. But you hear almost nothing about deaths from cars. (And by the way, humans kill about 1 million sharks every year.)

> **For generations now, we've prioritized the needs of automobiles, while ignoring the needs of all other modes of transportation such as bicyclists, pedestrians, and transit users.**
> — Charles T. Brown

Same time, longer distance

Did the construction of all those roads actually lead to time savings? Well, no. Highways are continuously expanded, with the idea that more space allows cars to move more freely. However, this extra space attracts more cars, leading to an increase in traffic volume. In effect, you end up with more road surface occupied by more cars. And all these cars ultimately need to enter cities, creating a bottleneck effect.

You are not stuck in traffic, you are traffic.
— TomTom[5]

In 1972, Alexander Szalai conducted an international study on time use, which also measured travel time. By then, the cars had become faster, which allowed people to cover distances more quickly. Surprisingly, Szalai concluded that we didn't reduce our travel time but instead spent the same time to travel further. More roads led to more cars, and faster cars led to more travel.

The invasion of the parking lots

Cars spend 95% of their time parked somewhere. It is estimated that the USA has 8 parking spaces for every vehicle. In 1920, cities first began to establish standards related to cars, from the width of the streets to the dimensions of a parking space. Licenses were issued for private parking lot operators.

In Los Angeles, for every 100 acres of land, there are 16 acres of parking lots. And not only that — the minimum requirements for how many parking spaces there must be per residence or business keep growing. In the '50s and '60s, this led to the construction of the iconic overhanging Dingbat apartments: cars could be parked under them. This was a good strategy when only 1 parking space was required per apartment, but when the minimum requirement became more than 1 space, other solutions had to be found. Parking spaces under residential buildings became giant puzzles. The necessity of the parking spaces dictated where support pillars were placed and, eventually, what buildings looked like.

5 → Originally a campaign in 2010 by Dutch satnav maker TomTom, but adopted by cyclists worldwide.

In the end, more mandatory parking spaces per residence also means that fewer homes can be built on the same plot of land. This adds to housing shortages, rising house prices and gentrification of neighbourhoods.

Taking Back Public Space

Parking places are exclusively for car owners. Or, as a cyclist, can I also use that space? Others wondered about this as well.

In 2005, Rebar, an art/design group from San Francisco, paid to use a parking space for an entire day and set it up with grass patches, plants, and benches. When their parking ticket expired, they packed their belongings and went home. Social media picked up on it, and the 'parklet' phenomenon spread.

In 2017, Brenda Puech from Hackney, London, applied to rent a parking space for a year to create a parklet. Her request was denied; a parklet does not meet the purpose of a parking space. "I'll do it anyway," she thought, and created a parklet outside her house. Initially, Puech was told to remove her parklet, but the neighbourhood supported her, and enormously successful petitions followed. As a consequence, Hackney became the first borough in the world to start an online application system for parklets.

Public spaces in cities and kerbsides should be for people, not just for storage of private, stationary metal boxes. — Brenda Puech

If you don't have cars in the city

In a story I came across online, someone talked about how work was carried out on their street. Due to a mix-up at the city office, the 'road closed' signs weren't taken down after the work was done. The effect was that the whole street came to life. Kids were playing in the street, and folks started hanging out outside together.

In 1989, a big earthquake on California's Central Coast had disastrous consequences. It also knocked down the Embarcadero Freeway in San Francisco. The city decided not to rebuild the freeway; instead, the space was turned into a pedestrian-friendly boulevard by the water. It quickly turned into one of the hottest spots in town. It was one of the first prominent examples of how removing a highway can change a city. Now, cities worldwide are tearing down highways and making streets car-free to reconnect neighbourhoods and people.

In 2019, Oslo, Norway, achieved 'Vision Zero' — a year with no fatal traffic accidents, the worst accident being someone who drove into a fence. Several measures were taken to achieve this success. For starters, more than 1000 parking spots were removed from the streets and more pedestrian and cycling paths were added to the existing ones. Public transport could count on a hefty investment and streets around elementary schools were closed off to traffic completely. As a result, the city centre became more vibrant, with an increase in visitors. Major brands were eager to locate their flagship stores in these car-free areas, and there was a renewed interest in city living.

When Ljubljana, Slovenia, made its city centre car-free in 2007, only 40% of residents supported the idea. A decade later, 97% are opposed to allowing cars back in. The city of Pontevedra in Spain also transitioned to a car-free city. The mayor who initiated this change has been re-elected more than 4 times.

THE CAR FREE CITY EFFECT

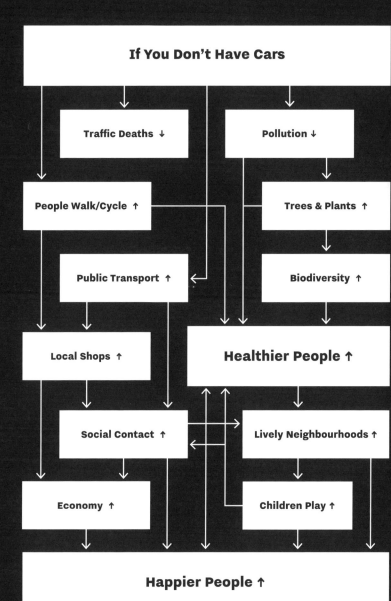

If You Don't Have Cars

Traffic Deaths ↓

Pollution ↓

People Walk/Cycle ↑

Trees & Plants ↑

Public Transport ↑

Biodiversity ↑

Local Shops ↑

Healthier People ↑

Social Contact ↑

Lively Neighbourhoods ↑

Economy ↑

Children Play ↑

Happier People ↑

It's not my duty as Mayor to make sure you have a parking spot. For me it's the same as if you bought a cow, or a refrigerator, and then asked me where you're going to put them.

— Miguel Lores

Over in Paris's 14th arrondissement, locals call themselves 'Hypervoisins' (hyper-neighbours). They organized a street dinner on Rue de l'Aude, with a table that was 215 metres long — reclaiming the street from the cars, for the neighbourhood. Residents say that, since the hypervoisins initiative, there's much more social interaction in the neighbourhood. People say 'bonjour' on the streets again when they run into each other.

As the car-free experiments highlight, cars have an enormous impact on public space, considering the number of people they transport. Of course, what makes a city liveable is different for everyone. A car-free city isn't very handy for, for example, plumbers who need to drive around with a van full of tools or people who have to get up early for a morning shift in a factory or nursing home. Some people actually need cars for their jobs (and I'm not talking about CEOs here). Making a city car-free inevitably impacts neighbourhoods — often leading to gentrification. Everything comes at a price.

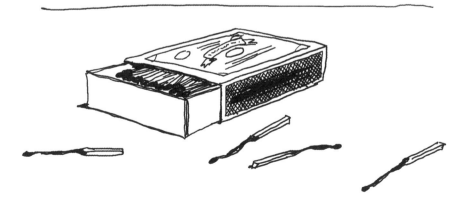

The Inefficient Food System

Now, let's focus on another sector that affects us all: food. We could talk about how much water it takes to produce an avocado (200 litres per 100 grams) or a cappuccino (200 litres - and if you skip the milk and have black coffee, it's still 140 litres). But let's just address the cow in the room: meat!

Meat Is Business

In children's books about farms, we typically see a happy cow (says 'moo'), a friendly pig (says 'oink'), and a playful chicken (says 'cluck cluck'). In the supermarket, the dairy and meat isles show us contented grazing animals. My personal favourite is the pig dressed as a butcher. He stands cheerfully at the butcher's shop, holding a knife, happy to chop up his fellow pigs and himself. These types of images tell us that meat comes from happy animals raised on charming little farms.

In the quest for optimal efficiency after WWII, the number of farming businesses decreased while the remaining businesses grew considerably. In this process, farms were caught between the pressure of bank loans to expand, and the supermarkets' demands to deliver as cheaply as possible. This quickly created a downward spiral: to cover costs, farmers have to produce more meat, grow more, borrow more, and then cover even more expenses. Supermarkets don't pay them enough while offering us cheap meat — meant to lure us in.

> [Food is] by far the most powerful medium available to us for thinking and acting together to change the world for the better.
> — Carolyn Steel

DISTRIBUTION OF MAMMALS ON EARTH

Mammal Biomass Measured in Tonnes of Carbon, 2015

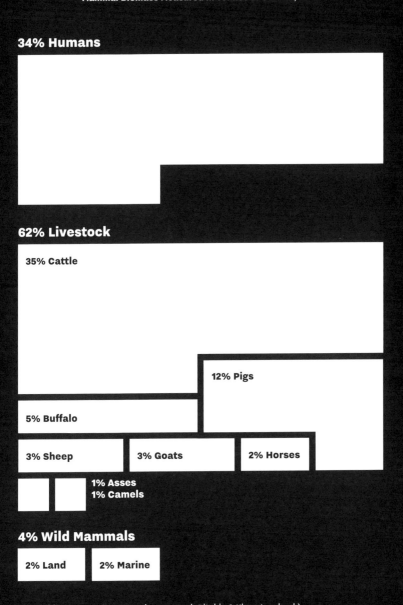

34% Humans

62% Livestock

35% Cattle

12% Pigs

5% Buffalo

3% Sheep

3% Goats

2% Horses

1% Asses
1% Camels

4% Wild Mammals

2% Land

2% Marine

Currently, only 4% of all mammal biomass[6] on Earth consists of wild animals. 34% of mammal biomass are humans, and 62% are livestock. Here are some more numbers: in 2020, more than 80 billion land animals (and 2000 billion fish) were slaughtered. You don't have to be a math genius to realize that all this livestock can't be kept on cute little farms with happily frolicking animals.

Thanks to the invention of Vitamin D and antibiotics, animals no longer have to go outside. Instead, they are often crammed together (efficiently) in dark barns, where they lead miserable lives until they're slaughtered after an even more miserable journey to the slaughterhouse.

Working in an abattoir is a shock... it's also a reminder: the biggest way that we interact with animals today is by eating them.

— Henry Mance

---

6 → The weight of living things — how researchers measure the mass of organims in an ecosystem.

Almost 77% of all agricultural land is used for producing animal feed. This makes livestock farming the leading cause of the destruction of ancient forests, including their biodiversity and the habitats of indigenous people. And all that livestock produces at least 14% of all greenhouse gases worldwide.

Is there anything good that comes from all this? Is there at least enough to eat for everyone? Sadly, no. According to the Food and Agriculture Organization of the UN, in 2022, between 691 and 783 million people worldwide went hungry. And in 2021, 42% of the world population were unable to afford a healthy diet. Meanwhile, during the COVID-19 crisis (2020-2022), the largest food corporations reported record profits.

The question that future generations will ask is: why did homo sapiens manage to build and maintain an infrastructure that, during the covid crisis, made the rich even richer while the poor became poorer? — Kiza Magendane

The IAASTD — an agriculture and science project of the World Bank — reported in 2016: "Agriculture is producing more food than ever before, both in total numbers as well as on a per capita basis, despite the fact that world population is growing. If harvests were used entirely and as effectively as possible as food, they could already feed 12 to 14 billion people today."

So, if we have enough food, why are people still going hungry? Because the production of meat eats up way more food than it gives back. A kilo of chicken needs two kilos of grain as food. A typical chicken farm takes 5 kilos of grain from the world market and only gives back 1 chicken in return. 1 kilo of beef requires 25 kilos of food. Consider those numbers when you know that, for poorer countries, 1 kilo of grain is way more valuable than 500 grams of chicken breast or 40 grams of beef.

According to Oxfam, 90% of the global grain trade is in the hands of just 4 big companies.[7] They're all about business: the grain goes to whoever pays the most. Rich countries buy it for animal feed, while people in poorer countries sometimes resort to eating mud to fill their empty stomachs. Meanwhile, all that food gobbled up by livestock turns into a bit of meat and dairy, but mostly it ends up as waste — yep, poop and pee — which means CO_2.

In fact, if you compare how much CO_2 is produced per type of protein, the results could not be any clearer: for each gram of chicken or milk protein, 10 times more CO_2 is produced than for each gram of bean protein. And for beef, it's a whopping 80 times more. And no — we don't actually need to eat that much meat. Purely from a health perspective, it has long been known that especially processed meats do nothing for a healthy body, and that consumption of red meat is known for producing higher LDL-cholesterol levels. Of course, the meat industry will only tell you about the benefits of consuming meat.

Soy is (not) for vegans

According to the WWF, between 2005 and 2017, about 5 million hectares of tropical forest (roughly the size of Slovakia) were chopped down each year to make way for farmland. Germany, Italy, Spain, the UK, and the Netherlands were responsible for 80% of the import of products linked to this deforestation. The top import product? Soy.

Originally, soy was grown for its oil, which is used in food and cosmetics. But then it was discovered that the leftover soy meal (or soy cake) makes perfect animal food because of its protein composition. Out of the soybean, 18.5% is used for oil, while 78.5% is crushed, and along with the 1% hulls (shells), it's turned into feed for livestock. This means that there is 2% waste. This might sound like a sustainable affair, until you realize that 75% of all soy cultivation goes straight to intensive

7 → The ABCD traders: Archer Daniels Midland (ADM), Bunge, Cargill and Louis Dreyfus

THE FOOD CHAIN

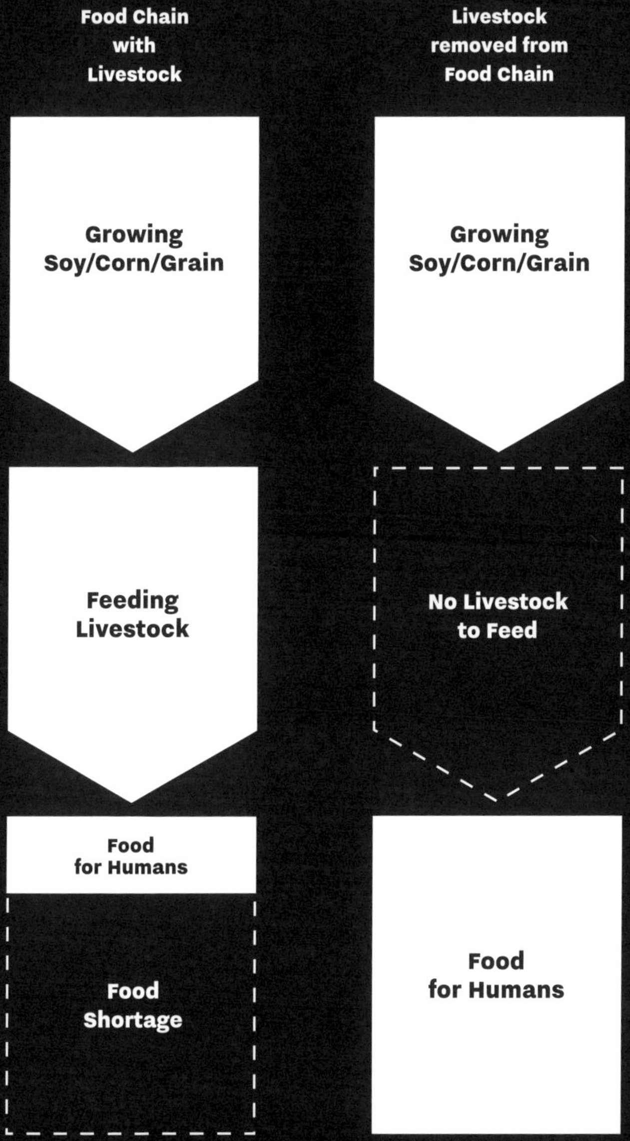

Food Chain
with
Livestock

Livestock
removed from
Food Chain

Growing
Soy/Corn/Grain

Growing
Soy/Corn/Grain

Feeding
Livestock

No Livestock
to Feed

Food
for Humans

Food
Shortage

Food
for Humans

animal farming. Soy production for human consumption has basically become an afterthought. This means that the livestock industry is the main reason most soy farmers grow soybeans at all — and the reason why tropical forests are being chopped down for their farmland.

> **Whether you eat meat or not, you can be part of this decision to limit the meat industry destroying our planet's resources.**
> — Stella McCartney

If you don't eat meat

Meat is often presented as the default or key ingredient in many meals, and indulging in a lot of meat is commonly seen as a sign of luxury. The meat industry loves this portrayal of its product because it keeps their business booming. The fact that so many people are starving and that natural habitats and biodiversity are disappearing; that there's too much nitrogen; that farmers are getting a raw deal; and that animals are suffering horribly — that's just collateral damage.

It is difficult to change any system, and especially when it's firmly in place. But it's not as difficult as it seems. If everyone switched to a plant-based diet and stopped eating meat, it would lead to a 75% reduction in climate-warming emissions, water pollution, and land use. And if we can also tackle the food waste problem — we throw away a shocking 30% of our food — then the world's food production could even go completely organic.

The future of farming

Many farmers are already shifting to more sustainable farming methods. They no longer have to buy enormous amounts of resources and use fewer machines; they prefer to let nature do some of the work. This approach promotes biodiversity and turns farms into habitats for various animals, insects, and plants. But while these, usually, small farms are better for nature, they are also more expensive to run — and the price of their produce will reflect that.

This brings up the issue of green privilege. For people who are barely scraping by, the production method of their food is not a priority. If you have to rely on a food bank for your dinner, you're not worried about whether the carrots or chicken breast are organic, you're just happy to have some.

We need to ask ourselves whether it is truly better to only have small farms, or whether it represents more of a romanticized ideal? These smaller farms are not particularly efficient when it comes to land use.

What, then, about environmentally friendly intensive farming? This can actually be done with innovative techniques (such as laser-based pest control instead of insecticides). Innovative and energy-efficient greenhouses, for instance, can yield a much bigger harvest while they use less land than sustainable but more traditional small farms. And if less land is needed for food production, more land can be restored to its natural state, and develop a flourishing biodiversity.

Perhaps the answer lies somewhere in the middle: a farming method that incorporates all good qualities from small-scale, innovative, and intensive agriculture.

However food is produced, it always has to be transported. On average, food travels 2,000 km(!) from its source to your plate. An employee at the IGA grocery store in Saint-Laurent, Canada, had a brilliant thought: "Could we reduce that distance to 0 kilometres?" It turns out that they could: the store's rooftop was transformed into a professional organic vegetable farm of approximately 2,300 square metres. It grows 30 kinds of vegetables and also contains beehives that produce about 500 jars of honey per year. The store efficiently uses water from its dehumidification system to water the crops. The green roof also helps to cool the building and its surrounding environment. This initiative seems to offer nothing but advantages: vegetables no longer need to be transported to the store, there is a new habitat for birds and insects, and on top of that (pun intended), this farm/store construction truly optimizes land use and infrastructure.

Chef's foodprint

In 2004, rising star René Redzepi became the chef and co-founder of the now world-famous Danish restaurant Noma. "Why import the most expensive ingredients and products from all over the world just to cook the same stuff as all the other fancy restaurants around the globe?" Redzepi wondered. He decided to cook at the highest level using only Scandinavian (seasonal) products — a way of cooking known as 'a sense of time and place' that inspired chefs worldwide. Guests should be able to taste from the food where and in what season they are. The ingredients were local, but the guests came from all over the world — by airplane. An unforeseen side-effect to sustainable cooking.

> **It's not sustainable. Financially and emotionally, as an employer and as a human being, it just doesn't work.** — René Redzepi

20 years later, Redzepi decided to close Noma. Cooking at the highest level is incredibly labour-intensive — often involving dozens of unpaid interns working 70-hour weeks (not just at Noma, but at all major restaurants).

Redzepi also had Noma's carbon footprint calculated. It turned out that a meal at Noma had a carbon footprint three times larger than a meal cooked at home. Surprisingly, foraging — which sounds super eco-friendly — accounted for 7% of Noma's emissions due to the fuel used for the van.

You shouldn't just trust your gut feeling that local is always better. You have to examine your assumptions. — Joris Bijdendijk

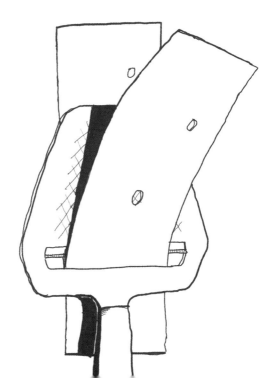

#5

REMOVE, DON'T ADD

When you try to find a solution to a problem, don't overcomplicate it. Sometimes, you can simply leave things out. When you scrap all that's not truly necessary, it will be easier to get back to the essence of the problem — and the solution.

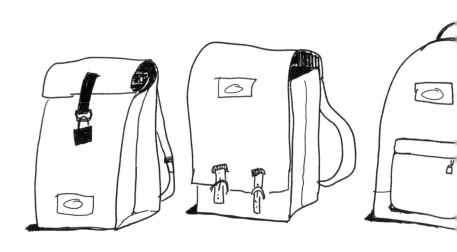

Monocultures

Cars, food, and bottled water are just the tip of the iceberg when it comes to the influence products have on our daily lives. These examples also show that a few large companies have a lot of power. These companies typically prioritise individual short-term interests (usually money) over collective long-term interests. To maximize profits and make production straightforward, they make their production processes as efficient and uniform as possible. As a result, everything looks the same — they have created monocultures.

Hazelnut Trees in Rows

The multinational Ferrero, manufacturer of Nutella, is considered a national treasure by Italians. Founded in 1946, Ferrero symbolizes Italy's post-war reconstruction. Pietro Ferrero first created Nutella as an alternative to chocolate, which was incredibly expensive after the war. He came up with a clever recipe containing hazelnuts, which have great nutritional value and were widely available in the region.

According to the BBC, Ferrero buys a quarter of the global hazelnut supply annually. To reduce dependence on foreign hazelnuts, Ferrero is expanding its own hazelnut plantations to 90,000 hectares. Italians are proud, and tourists love Nutella shops, but farmers are complaining: the hazelnut monoculture is harming biodiversity, turning the land into a desert. It's disastrous for the environment and, ironically, eventually for the monocultures themselves. Economically, monocultures seem logical: growing just one type of plant seems very efficient. And it is a very successful model, but (here we go again): only for the short term.

Agroforestry

Researchers from Wageningen University and Research (WUR) are studying monocultures. Hazelnut trees on a plantation are planted closely together in rows, while in nature they occur in forests. The hazelnut tree would perform much better in an agroforestry system — a form of agriculture where trees and plants are interspersed with crops, farming, or livestock. Agroforestry also improves resource efficiency: different crops complement and cooperate with each other. One plant has deep roots to draw up water, another provides shade, and a third releases nutrients into the soil for a fourth — just like nature has been doing for millions of years.

The WUR researchers are now working on small, lightweight robots that can make this type of farming easier with the help of Artificial Intelligence: farmers should be able to use them for sowing and harvesting different kinds of crops. The researchers are designing the robots in such a way that they should be affordable for small-scale farmers.

> **The fields will become smaller, with cultivation techniques that are both intensive and ecologically sound.** — Peter Groot Koerkamp

Sick Bananas

Did you know that people's DNA is 60% similar to bananas' DNA? Or that bananas are the world's most eaten and exported fruit? (Bananas are obviously hugely popular and have inspired many modern art works, too — you might have heard about the banana/duct tape incidents.)

99% of the bananas we eat are of the Cavendish variety. This was not always the case. In the 1950s, the Gros Michel was the most popular type of banana. But this variety was very vulnerable to a toxic fungal disease — Panama disease. The Cavendish proved to be much more resistant to it, so global logistics started catering to the Cavendish, from production to the size of the boxes. The Cavendish banana stays green during shipping and becomes a beautiful yellow in the supermarket, where it is sold below cost price to attracts customers.

Meanwhile, Panama disease has mutated, and the Cavendish banana is susceptible to its current variant. Now, each banana plant must be sprayed about 50 times a year with what is called 'crop protector'. Colombia has tens of thousands of hectares of plantations, all close together, with the same Cavendish bananas. If Panama disease reaches these plantations, the infection will spread very quickly.

The COVID-19 virus spread rapidly around the world in 2020. The only real way to control it (or really, slow it down a bit) was to limit physical contact between people — to keep some distance. Likewise, if we diversify the landscape, it will be harder for (plant) diseases to spread.

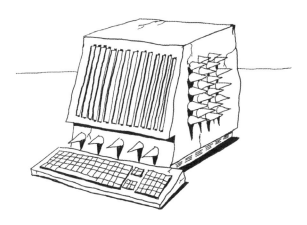

Monocultures Are Everywhere

Monocultures are not only found in agriculture, but also in design, architecture and technology. Computers, for instance, typically have the same operating systems and are, therefore, vulnerable, especially when interconnected. This observation was made by Stephanie Forrest, a professor of computer science and director of the Biodesign Center for Biocomputing,

Security and Society. In the early 1990s, she already drew parallels between Panama disease and computer viruses. In 1988, the first-ever computer worm, known as the Morris Worm, disabled 10% of all computers connected to the Internet within 24 hours. This worm was created by a student named Robert Morris, who mostly wanted to expose weaknesses in the emerging public Internet. In 2016, hackers using the Mirai Botnet — a collective of infiltrated computers functioning as a sort of supercomputer — managed to disrupt services of major platforms like Twitter, Netflix, and CNN.

Monocultures are dangerous in almost every facet of life.
— Fred B. Schneider

Ending up in design loops

In his 1995 essay 'The Generic City,' Rem Koolhaas observed that cities worldwide are all starting to look like each other. It's a trend that results in spaces full of soulless design. This uniformity spans from retail shops to street layouts, architectural styles, and even city skylines. French anthropologist Marc Augé identified a related concept he called 'non-places' — public areas where life is absent, and everyone is merely passing through, where functionality trumps living: shopping malls, airports, hotel rooms, and large movie theatres.

Brand strategist Axel Murrell also noted this homogeneity in his blog post 'The Age of Average'. He mentions that photos of many Airbnbs show a striking sameness in interior décor: white walls, brown or beige furniture of natural (or natural-looking) materials, and grey cushions. Wherever you go in the world, you will most likely recognise a coffee shop by its wooden bars, trendily tattooed baristas, and the riso prints on the walls. Even museum gift shops have a uniform appearance. Corporate logos have shifted towards a universal sans-serif font style. Plastic surgeons offer standardised packages leading to uncannily similar-looking influencers who all have a bio like 'Love to travel and see new places, be yourself'. The craft beer scene is no different — there are hipster microbreweries around every corner, always producing an edgy yet fruity IPA. Cheers! (I love IPA by the way.)

It seems that the drive for economic efficiency has deeply infiltrated our everyday lives, influencing our thought processes and stifling creativity. For that, diversity might just be the best remedy.

Diversity creates dimension in the world.
— Elizabeth Ann Lawless

Diversity is always a healthy element. In 2020, the University of Cambridge decided not to mow a lawn at King's College — a 'green desert' the size of half a soccer field — for the first time since 1772. Instead, they sowed the seeds of 33 local flower species. Later, 84 types of flower species were counted, and insects returned as well.

Everything is interconnected. Diversity attracts and fosters life in all kinds of ways. It works the same way in your personal life. If you only know 1 type of person from 1 type of neighbourhood or 1 type of background, you will find yourself in a monoculture, too.

#6

CREATIVITY NEEDS DIVERSITY

Because we all use the same tools and networks for inspiration, our solutions often end up looking the same. To break free from the creative loop, try using tools you wouldn't typically use. Collaborate with people who have different skills or perspectives. Diversify your toolkit and find the loopholes.

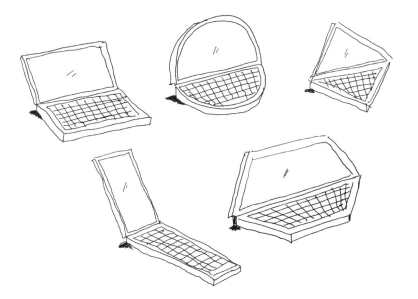

INTO THE FUTURE

THE MINDSET

People don't need
enormous cars; they need
admiration and respect.
They don't need a constant
stream of new clothes;
they need to feel that
others consider them to be
attractive, and they need
excitement and variety and
beauty. People don't need
electronic entertainment;
they need something
interesting to occupy their
minds and emotions. And
so forth. Trying to fill real
but nonmaterial needs —
for identity, community,

self-esteem, challenge, love, joy — with material things is to set up an unquenchable appetite for false solutions to never-satisfied longings. A society that allows itself to admit and articulate its nonmaterial human needs, and to find nonmaterial ways to satisfy them, would require much lower material and energy throughputs and would provide much higher levels of human fulfilment.

— Donella H. Meadows[1]

1 → Limits to Growth: The 30-Year Update

Power and Pitfalls of Simplifying

At a symposium, young German writer Valentina Vapaux (2003) was asked, "Why do young people do so little?" She replied, "You complain about how stupid young people are, but we didn't create this world."

Each generation appears to shift the responsibility for their actions to the next. We'd rather enjoy life right now without having to think about future problems and instead choose to buy the stuff we want — if we can. In the 1980s, capitalism reached star status with the release of the movie 'Wall Street'. It was intended as criticism of the greed-is-good society, but it had an unintended side effect: main character Gordon Gekko became the personification of unbridled capitalism and a role model for a new generation of money chasers.

Tragedy of the Commons

People often take as much as they can, even if it negatively impacts society as a whole, and ultimately themselves — they're not exactly great long-term thinkers. An example is the fisherman: for an individual fisherman, it's more profitable to catch as much tuna as possible. However, if he catches it faster than the tuna can repopulate, there will be no tuna left to catch eventually — and thus, no income. Plus, the absence of tuna in the ocean will affect the rest of the ecosystem. So, in the long run, it's smarter not to overfish.

But this fisherman can't do this alone — his colleagues need to join in, and they all need to trust each other. What if some of them continue to catch as much tuna as they can? Then, even if the others hold back, the sea will still be depleted anyway. So, should everyone just take what they can? Or should they try to build the trust needed and work together? This type of dilemma was discussed by American ecologist Garrett Hardin in his article 'The Tragedy of the Commons'.

Ruin is the destination toward which all men rush, each pursuing his own best interest in a society that believes in the freedom of the commons. Freedom in a commons brings ruin to all. — Garrett Hardin

Shifting Baseline Syndrome

Thinking long-term is difficult because we don't experience everything first-hand: what we grow up with and live through seems normal to us. That's why we don't really think much about the gradual decline of nature either; because we barely even notice it happening during our lifetime.

For grandma, the sea was teeming with 200 fish while our parents thought the sea was full of life with 100 fish. We've only ever known the sea with 50 fish, while our kids are used to just 25 fish — and they think that's plenty. But grandma wouldn't recognize the sea today. This is what is known as shifting baseline syndrome. Each generation uses its own situation as a reference point, and because environmental changes happen gradually, we don't really 'see' them. So, it's important to look across generations if you want to spot the changes.

Versus vs. Not-Versus

In the 1950s, the American political scientist Herbert Simon introduced the concept of bounded rationality: the idea that it is impossible for humans to have all the facts necessary to make optimal decisions. It's easier for us to use other methods to think about decisions, like metaphors or simple contrasts: good vs. bad / global vs. local / big vs. small / centralized vs. decentralized / short term vs. long term / right vs. left.

These kinds of contrasts imply that if you're not in favour of something, you're automatically against it. But the world is more complex than that. What do you really know for sure? And where does your information come from?

SHIFTING BASELINE

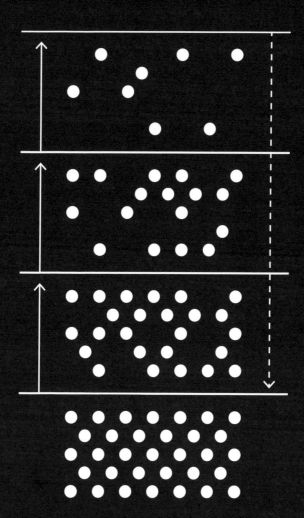

Ask critical questions and actively seek out information that doesn't match what you already know (or think you know). Consider your confirmation bias: the tendency we all have to search for or interpret information in a way that confirms our own beliefs. (This book is full of 'em.)

Who determines what you know?

Be aware of algorithms — as soon as they learn what you like to view or read, they will show you more of the same type of content. Before you know it, you'll be caught in an information bubble. What would Ada Lovelace think of this use of her invention?

The media have quite some tricks to make us consume their content. For instance, they love to use those contrasts mentioned above, like right vs. left, or city vs. countryside. These are too simple to represent how the world works, which is exactly why people like them: they're easy. They seem to bring some clarity to their world. And because people like them, they sell — which is why the media use them. Keep that in mind next time you come across a sensational headline.

PERCY IS A HUMAN!!!

A good example is what happened with Freshii, a Canadian restaurant chain. Customers who checked out at the self-service counter were assisted by a virtual cashier. The issue was that these cashiers weren't virtual at all; they were real people who dialled in from low-wage countries and were paid far less than the Canadian minimum wage. A journalist for the Toronto Star wrote an article about it, sparking controversy.

There are thousands of call centre workers in low-wage countries. But we —usually— don't see them. In the Freshii case, suddenly, cheap labour was given a face. This led to a heated debate over low wages and exploitation.

Percy was removed from Freshii restaurants, resulting in the 'Percy' workers having to look for new jobs, perhaps in other call centres. Places where they aren't seen by the Western consumer, but where they still work for them. What then, has actually improved? There might be more awareness now, but in practice, little seems to have truly changed — and for the workers who got fired, nothing improved at all. Quite likely, their situations were made worse. So, how do we effectively change something in the ways companies work?

Ignoring vs. Joining vs. Alternatives vs. Activism

Large corporations like insurance companies and pension providers make money through their shareholdings in the fossil industry. As shareholders, they are part-owners and have a say in the fossil companies' policies.

With growing criticism of the polluting fossil industry, it is becoming more common for major shareholders to pull out of the fossil industry. While a pull-out is a strong statement, this also means that these companies lose any influence they might have had, and their former shares are immediately bought by other investors (or repurchased by the company). And the fossil company continues as usual.

Activist investor groups like Follow This don't pull out — they buy in: they deliberately buy shares in a company to gain a say and thus influence policy. Follow This has members who each own 1 share in companies like Shell, BP, Total, ExxonMobil, or Chevron. At every shareholders' meeting, Follow This represents its members and consistently submits climate resolutions — which are gaining increasing support from other big investors.

If you believe in this philosophy of internal change, you might also wonder if working for a fossil company could be more effective than protesting — by changing the company from within. In such a case, you would need to find quite a few allies within the company, and you'd need to be ready to play the long game. And that's challenging, considering people don't change quickly, especially if they personally benefit from the status quo. But if you try, you might succeed.

A different way to change something in an industry is to become a competitor who, quite simply, does it better. For example, by founding a company based on co-operatives (where each employee is also a shareholder). Another format that allows companies to focus on their own goals (like sustainability or paying fair prices to farmers) is to operate as a stewardship. This means that certain core values can be ingrained in the company's DNA and can never be influenced by shareholders... But I don't see the oil companies becoming co-ops or stewardships anytime soon.

A lot of people are dependent on the fossil industry in one way or another. That's why it's hard to change it. But sooner or later, renewable energy will take over — and fossil energy companies as well as activists also know that. That's why many activists are not asking for a total and immediate end to the existence of energy companies; but they do want subsidies for the fossil industry to stop, and they want a rapid transition to green energy. Why wait?

Activist groups like Extinction Rebellion and Just Stop Oil take direct action: they call attention to the destruction caused by the fossil industry through civil disobedience — they make noise in the public sphere. This type of activism has multiple goals: to make politics take action, to exert social pressure on the fossil industry, and to make people aware of the urgency of the matter.

Disco inferno

The Burning Man art festival, which originally started on the beaches of San Francisco, has grown into an event attracting 80,000 visitors in Black Rock desert. The profile of the attendees has also changed: with its success, the festival now attracts many wealthy individuals. These affluent guests often arrive in private planes. Because of the 'need' for an airport and various power and water supplies, the festival now has a carbon footprint of 100,000 tons of CO_2.[2] That's why, in 2023, climate activists blocked the road to the festival. They were forcefully removed, but poetic justice was served a few days later: a torrential downpour turned the entire event into a muddy hell.

I had thought that climate change was a distant threat. I thought that the grown-ups had it all under control.

— Phoebe Plummer

One or the other

What can we do to change how our economy works? Activism alone is not enough. We need a more fundamental approach. Some people argue that progress through innovation will save us. On the other hand, there are those who believe that we need to radically simplify our lifestyle as quickly as possible — and end the constant pursuit of growth. Which is the best solution?

2 → That is the same as 22,000 gas powered cars produce in a year.

Degrowth Is Growing

Economic recessions are always good for nature. Less money is spent, and therefore, less is produced, which ultimately benefits the Earth. The Degrowth movement proposes a controlled recession in which the economy stabilizes and the world "prioritizes social and ecological well-being instead of corporate profits, over-production and excess consumption."

By the way, Degrowthers are not a bunch of gloomy pessimists. The 'de' in 'Degrowth' might sound negative, but when you understand the origin of the term, you will see that it's not: it comes from the French 'la décroissance' and Italian 'la decrescita', which both describe a river returning to its normal state after a huge flood. So, degrowth isn't about pessimistic shrinkage, but about a normalisation of the economy which makes it possible to operate within the Earth's capacity limits.

The Degrowth movement is an ambitious one. Their goals are to "reduce less-necessary production, improve public services, introduce a green jobs guarantee, reduce working hours, enable sustainable development". Life is about more than just chasing immense material wealth at the expense of everything and everyone. True wealth lies in being content with less materialistic stuff. This doesn't mean that Degrowth is only about 'less' and 'sacrifice', but also about 'more': a better quality of life, for example. This can be achieved by making choices that make not just you, but everyone happier — like a 4-day workweek, for instance. Various studies have shown that a 4-day workweek leads to a much better work-life balance, increased productivity and more quality time.

These ideas about wealth and prosperity are gaining traction, which funnily enough means that the Degrowth movement itself is growing, including various spin-off movements. As the movement grows, so does the criticism of it. Degrowth is often labelled as a green privilege hobby: too idealistic and unrealistic. For instance, some hardcore Degrowthers believe that income disparities across the globe should be levelled. Worldwide, there are 650 million people living on about $2.15 a day. How do you convince the world's wealthy to share a significant portion of their income with the poor? When the only thing they'd get in return is less money for themselves and a reduction in other people's misery?

Unless someone like you cares a whole awful lot, nothing is going to get better. It's not.

— The Once-ler

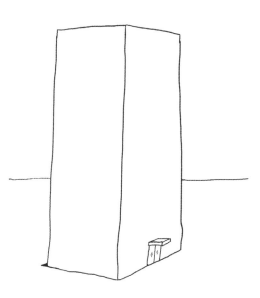

Innovation Will / Will Not Save Us

If everything was truly better in the past, we wouldn't have made any progress. Innovation has brought us microwaves and TikTok, but also antibiotics and computers. And let's not forget the dishwasher, which has prevented many a family argument.

Do not allow your mind to be imprisoned by majority thinking. Remember that the limits of science are not the limits of imagination.

— Patricia Bath

Since male engineers hadn't yet invented a good dishwasher in the late 19th century, Josephine Cochrane decided to take matters into her own hands. She believed that women had a better use for their time than washing dishes — and her machine would help with that. Her dishwasher hit the market in 1893 and gained a lot of attention at the World's Columbian Exposition, leading to orders from primarily hotels and restaurants. The machine was still too expensive for the average household, which was actually Cochrane's intended audience. It wouldn't be until the 20th century that the dishwasher became a common household appliance.

Another household invention with a big impact is the coffee filter. In 1908, Melitta Bentz did not enjoy the coffee grounds floating in her cup and decided to do something about it. She punched holes in a pot and used some blotting paper on top to create the first prototype. Not much later, she filed for a patent and founded her company Melitta.

The driving forces behind the birth control pill were — perhaps not surprisingly — also women: Margaret Sanger and Katharine McCormick. They believed that women, as the ones who get pregnant and have to deal with the (health) implications of pregnancy and childbirth, should have control over contraception. Sanger, a midwife and family planning activist, came up with the idea for the pill. McCormick, who was a suffragette, was one of the first women to study at MIT: she earned her bachelor's degree in biology in 1904. After the death of her husband, who left her a sizeable inheritance, she made a large investment to fund the development of the birth control pill by Gregory Goodwin Pincus. At the time, there were various laws against the use of condoms within marriage. Therefore, the research was conducted under the guise of a 'fertility treatment'. The result was Enovid, or the pill, which gave women much greater autonomy and sexual freedom, and consequently also had a huge social impact.

In the 20th century, many inventions had more impact than their creators initially expected. For instance, Kevlar (invented by Stephanie Kwolek) is used in a very diverse range of products. And the computerization of the telephone system (by Erna Schneider Hoover) was a huge step in communication technology.

Extra Energy

Since the industrial revolution, innovations have been made in rapid succession. Often, the effect and development of these innovations is initially underestimated. Current data show that the production of renewable energy even surpasses the most optimistic models of the IPCC. Right now, the biggest challenge in renewable energy is storage.

Often, one innovation leads to another at a rapid pace. That also means that technical innovations are advancing faster than politics can keep up with, and tech companies are ahead of government regulations. Some politicians — especially those who won their seats by saying that climate change is a hoax — are not very keen on addressing climate change or investing in renewable energy. But even when those politicians are part of the government, progressive companies continue to move forward with their energy transition. They know it's the future.

There is always a dark side

The country that produces more solar panels than anyone else is China. It produces 10 times more than Europe and the US combined and also is a major supplier of solar panel components. Unfortunately, according to reports, Uyghur forced labour is being used for the production of these parts and panels.

Even the best inventions can turn out to have a dark side. Humans often tend to use inventions without thinking, and to overuse them without thinking about the consequences.

In the 19th century, coal reserves were slowly running out in England. Innovation led to coal being used more efficiently, providing a higher return on investment than before. The result? Coal was now running out even faster. This paradox — that efficiency leads to lower utility costs, making it attractive to use more — was also observed by economist William Stanley Jevons. We've seen the same effect when more highways were constructed and cars got faster — it only attracted more cars and longer-distance travel (see page 99). Apparently, humans have the tendency to do things simply because they can.

JEVONS PARADOX

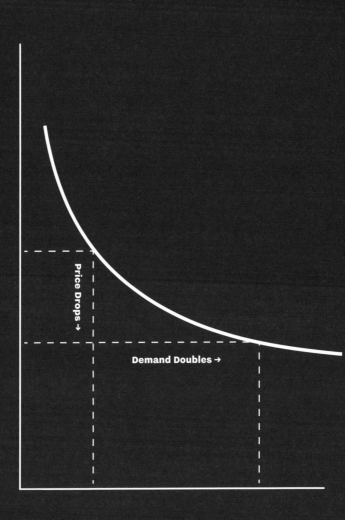

Let's Make It 'Sustainable'

Innovative technology made cars faster, more efficient, electric, but they also got bigger — and then some. A current Mini Cooper is one and a half times the size of the original version. By 2020, half of all 'sustainable' electric cars were SUVs. (Even Lego cars got bigger — from 4 bricks to 6 or 8 bricks wide.)

Larger cars also require larger batteries. An important component for those batteries is lithium along with cobalt, nickel, and manganese, which all have to be mined. About 80% of the lithium imported by the European Union comes from the Atacama Desert in Chile. There, pollution from mining has become a problem for the local population; they are paying the price for Europe's exploding demand for lithium. The same principle goes for the other raw materials: these are mostly mined in the global South, in communities that suffer because of the global North's growing demand.

> If we get to complete sustainability then, as observed, we have simply got to the point of being 100% less bad. Whatever form it takes, less bad is not the same as good.
> — William McDonough

Nothing stays in Chile; it all goes to other places. We don't have electric vehicles in Chile. We suffer from contamination, and the green energy goes to the Global North. But at whose cost?

— Lesley Muñoz Rivera

The idea "I'm driving emission-free, I've paid for it, so I'm doing my part" doesn't really hold up. It's CO_2 tunnel vision. An electric car is not good or 'better' for the planet. It is still bad, just a bit less so — it still needs energy to run. You might not see smoke coming out of your electric SUV, but know this: there was pollution involved in its production. You just didn't see it.

The idea that technical innovation will save the day is very appealing. And according to the World Economic Forum, technology can indeed help achieve the United Nations' sustainability goals. But the reality is that innovative technology is mostly used to turn a profit.

#7

CHANGE, DON'T REPLACE

When you want to make an improvement, don't simply replace something. Instead, ask yourself: why do I need this? The answer may well indicate that there may be a totally different way to fulfil your needs.

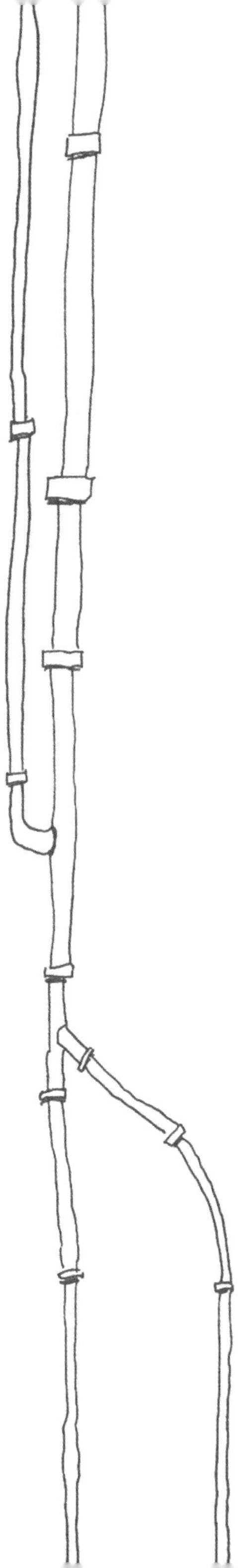

Degrowth + Innovation

Fashion/Art collective MSCHF made a microscopic Louis Vuitton handbag, measuring 657 by 222 by 700 micrometres (about the size of a bread crumb). In 2023, it was sold through an online auction for $63,750. Something valuable obviously doesn't have to be very big — or use a lot of resources.

Just because someone is opposed to unrestrained capitalist growth, that does not automatically mean that they are also against innovation or that they want the economy to shrink. Likewise, Degrowth and innovation are not necessarily opposing ideas. Perhaps we need them both.

You never change things by fighting the existing reality. To change something, build a new model that makes the existing model obsolete.

— Buckminster Fuller

HOW TO SAVE THE WORLD

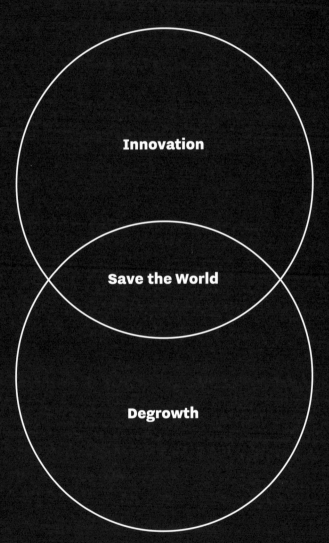

Law of the handicap of a head start

What good would Degrowth do in economically developing countries? Wouldn't they benefit more from innovation and products that allow them to raise their standards of living — but in a clean way? Innovation can help them develop their economies in a different, better way than the now-rich economies have done. With healthier food, better housing and more vegetation. In this context, the idea behind Degrowth — that more can be done with less resources — could help these emerging economies to develop better, cleaner and more future-proof systems than the rich countries currently have. With time, advancements in innovation are likely to give them an edge over the currently wealthy countries — who will have difficulty to pull out of their existing (polluting) systems.

Less private, more public

The Degrowth ideals actually combine very well with those of technological innovation: do more with less. Instead of manufacturing electric suvs, we could think about smarter public transport solutions. Take, for example, the autonomous shuttle buses developed by Finnish tech company Sensible 4. These self-driving buses are able to adjust their routes dynamically and pick up and drop off passengers anywhere. They have the same volume as an suv but can fit up to 10 people, which also adds a social element to the trip. With such innovations — and if we move away from the notion that everyone needs their own car — real structural changes in transportation can occur.

> A developed country is not a place where the poor have cars. It's where the rich use public transportation. — Gustavo Petro

SOLUTION

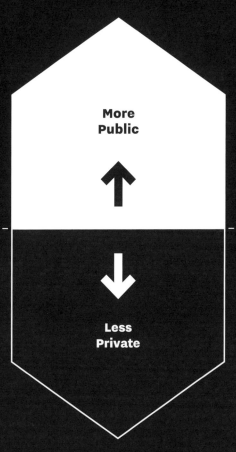

Sticky Trickle-Down

There's a theory that wealthy people let their money trickle down to the lower classes: the trickle-down effect, which is said to benefit everyone in all layers of society. Proponents of this theory, who include the shortest-serving Prime Minister of the UK ever, argue that the rich should not be taxed too heavily. Low taxes would make it easier for them to invest in private planes, super yachts, and space travel. The theory says that those investments create jobs and pay for the development of new technologies that will in the end be used for the greater good.

In practice, not much of the untaxed wealth seems to trickle down. The wealthy often invest in assets like housing. Which has an undesirable effect on the housing market: homes that were once affordable for the less wealthy are now out of their reach, forcing them to look for cheaper options in areas where they displace even less affluent groups. This domino effect continues, and a few steps down the line, nurses and teachers have to live outside the city where they work.

On balance, the result is that rich people float around in their super yachts or lounge around in their 4ᵗʰ house while the people who work for them can't even find or afford a first home. So in practice, the elite is sitting on a huge pile of money, eating their caviar on toast, while the world needs more money to innovate solutions to acute problems in the world.

A Little Bit More of Limitarianism

Economic Limitarianism is the idea that no one should be exceptionally rich. One of the major thinkers behind the theory is Belgian professor of Ethics Ingrid Robeyns.

INNOVATION CHAIN

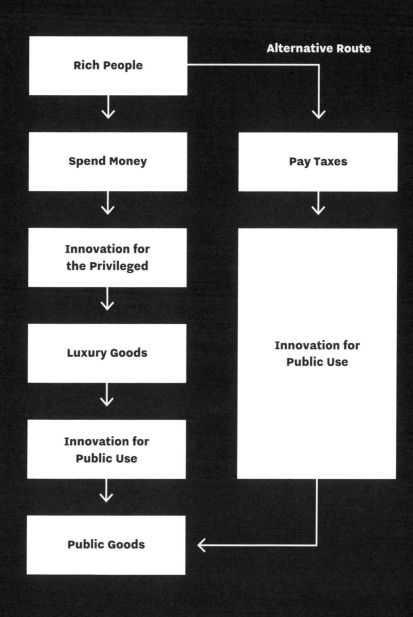

Limitarianism has no problems with private property and income inequality, but it does argue that you should put a limit on wealth that doesn't really add anything to your life.

> If you already have $10 million, it doesn't add much to your lifestyle if you get another 100,000 euros or dollars. But if you have no wealth at all, then any increase is significant. — Ingrid Robeyns

By taxing 100% above a certain level of wealth, 2 important issues would be addressed. Firstly, the financial means gathered from any extreme wealth tax enables the collective action needed to solve urgent issues. Secondly, it protects democracy by limiting ultra-rich people's influence on politics and society.

Right now, the ultra-rich do have that influence. Besides 'buying' politicians by supporting their campaigns (why is that even legal?), they can do and have done many other things that influence international politics. For example, they can buy an entire social network; or decide whether a besieged country has, or does not have, access to the Internet (now "let that sink in"). The question is: exactly how much wealth makes someone 'just rich' and what makes them 'extremely rich'? And: should such an extreme wealth tax also apply to corporations? But above all, how do you make it happen?

Progressive politicians who want to implement an extreme wealth tax are stuck with other, 'sort-of-progressive' and conservative politicians who are influenced by wealthy people and large corporations. No government wants to implement real drastic measures — in terms of taxes or environmental policies — because that is political suicide. After all, politicians usually want to be re-elected. Nevertheless, there are also positive developments.

When we say 'tax the rich,' we mean nesting-doll yacht rich. For-profit prison rich. Betsy DeVos, student-loan-shark rich. Trick-the-country-into-war rich. Subsidizing-workforce-with-food-stamps rich. Because that kind of rich is simply not good for society, and it's like 10 people — Alexandria Ocasio-Cortez

Effective Altruism

Some very wealthy individuals are no longer willing to wait for government policies. They have started initiatives to structurally donate their money for the greater good. They often do this united in networks — as wealthy people tend to enjoy those. Examples include The Patriotic Millionaires and Giving What We Can. The Patriotic Millionaires advocate for a fair tax system, a liveable minimum wage, and equal political representation. They have even published books detailing how the rich manipulate the economy and politics to become even wealthier. At Giving What We Can, members pledge to donate a certain amount of their income or wealth annually according to the principles of Effective Altruism — a movement aimed at saving as many people as possible in the most efficient way. They donate to causes that, according to scientific research, will have the most impact. With sophisticated websites, they track the results and get to feel like investors whose return on investment is a better world.

Give and let go

Critics point out that this type of donation might interfere with government-regulated organizations. It is a kind of "I'll help you, but then I'll tell you how to do it"-aid.

There is a different way to help — with no strings attached. Banksy did the following: he sent an email to human rights activist Pia Klemp, who was rescuing refugees with boats. It read: "Hello Pia, I've read about your story in the papers. You sound like a badass. I am an artist from the UK and I've made some work about the migrant crisis, obviously I can't keep the money. Could you use it to buy a new boat or something? Please let me know. Well done. Banksy." A new boat was bought with the money, and it was named after Louise Michel, a French teacher and anarchist. Banksy painted it pink and added a signature image of a girl in a life vest, holding a heart-shaped buoy.

> **We are Anarchists because it is absolutely impossible to obtain justice for all in any other way than by destroying institutions founded on force and privilege.** — Louise Michel

Longtermism: the Multibillionaire Space Race

Some of the wealthiest among us have their own philosophy about how to save humanity: longtermism, a concept that stems from Effective Altruism. This movement believes that the best way to save the most lives is to focus on the distant future; in other words, they focus on saving all the people who are yet to be born. That, from now until the Earth ceases to be habitable, could be as many as one quadrillion people (that's a 1 with 15 zeros). Some longtermists then took this idea further: they want to ensure that humanity doesn't end with the death of our planet, but continues somewhere in outer space...

And there you have them: the 'Space Barons'! Elon Musk, Jeff Bezos, and third wheel Richard Branson. All 3 are heavily invested in their space programs. With millions of fans (I once wrote something critical about Musk on LinkedIn, and the number of angry comments was astounding) and billions of dollars, they are shaping the future of space travel. Their goal is not just to colonize Mars but all of space; they call it the 'new frontier'. But let's be honest: colonizing Earth wasn't exactly an unqualified success in retrospect. And while space travel is cool and interesting, it also detracts attention from what is relevant on Earth, now — especially for those who will not have a yacht to live on when the sea level rises.

The space programs of the super-rich are not just there to save the world or humanity, either: often, they're another instrument to make money. Nowadays, there are so many commercial satellites from companies like Starlink and Amazon that they are literally getting in the way of scientists' view of space — who now struggle to detect meteorites that could threaten Earth.

> As fantastical as America's space ambitions might have seemed, sending a man into space was starting to feel like a straightforward task compared to putting black and white students together in the same Virginia classrooms.
> — Margot Lee Shetterly

Proxima Centauri b

Humans might be able to establish a settlement on Mars, but then what? There's not much else there. The nearest Earth-like planet that might be habitable for humans is Proxima Centauri b, which orbits the red dwarf star Proxima Centauri. It is about 4.2 light-years away, meaning that even with the best, state-of-the-art technology we currently have, it would still take about 6,300 years to get there. So, perhaps the 250-times-great-grandchildren of the original crew would arrive, which means that we would have to select enough people to ensure they don't succumb to the many risks of inbreeding over so many generations. Just as a sidenote, it would be convenient for the crew to be vegan — or they will have to bring livestock along on the journey.

Another sidenote: we don't even know whether people could actually survive on Proxima Centauri b, so all these hypothetical efforts might be in vain.

For now, longtermism seems more like a convenient excuse to organize space trips for the super-rich. "I want to thank every Amazon employee and every Amazon customer because you guys paid for all this." With these words, Bezos (along with an 18-year-old rich kid who received a ticket worth millions from daddy) embarked on an 11-minute journey into space.

We want to thank Jeff Bezos for going to space, because while he was up there... we were organizing a union.
— Chris Smalls

The issue is that these people, who — with their wealth and re-sources— could solve many urgent problems, are instead competing over whose ideas are better for longtermism and, primarily, whose rocket is launched into space first. It is basically a very costly billionaire pissing contest. Wouldn't it be better if they just paid taxes? They could even compete over who pays the most.

The greatest threat to our planet is the belief that someone else will save it. — Robert Swan

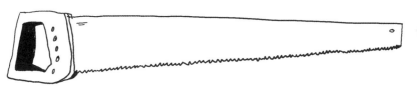

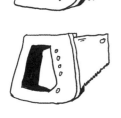

Rethinking Creating

Back to Earth. What can you personally do for the (near) future? The reality is that there's an inherent tension between what you'd like to do in an ideal world and the fact that you also need to pay your rent. As a creative, you're simply not always in a position to make the 'right' choices. And we won't save the world by starting 'green design agencies' because even if you start one with the best intentions, do your clients share those?

Political economists Rosie Collington and Mariana Mazzucato have shown that 'green' consultancy firms often face conflicts of interest — for example, when some of their clients don't really care about the environment but just want to check the 'I'm green' box for their brand. While a green report creates the illusion that a company is doing the environmentally responsible thing, it is rarely fully implemented in practice.

You can also consider this principle for you as a creative: are you simply checking the 'I'm green' box or have you really changed your mindset and behaviour? Let's have a look at what we can do within the creative industry. In the end, we're still creators, but we have a lot of new knowledge that can help us make better choices. No greenwashing, but real change.

Human Centred → Eco Centred

When designing products and solutions, the focus is usually on the interests of humans. While this is not surprising, this focus also means that the design process has no regard for the consequences for other species — or even other people (like people in different places or circumstances). To prevent this from happening, we need to anticipate these consequences in the design process. For example: when designing a car-free city, take it a step further than just designing it for people — design it for all forms of life. After all, we are part of an ecosystem. We can design with that in mind, shifting from human-centred to eco-centred design.

HUMAN CENTRED / ECO CENTRED

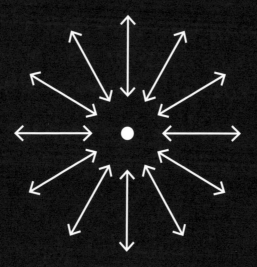

Human Centred

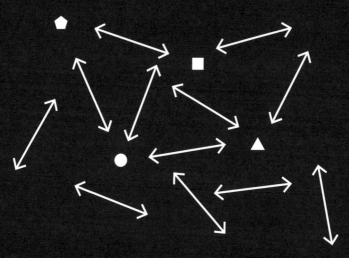

Eco Centred

Let us not forget that design is a noun as well as a verb, a product as well as a process. It involves the entire process of design, production, delivery, as well as the afterlife of products. Every one of the stages of the design process involves not only people but also resources, both natural and manmade and which directly or indirectly may impact the entire ecosystem.

— Janak Mistry

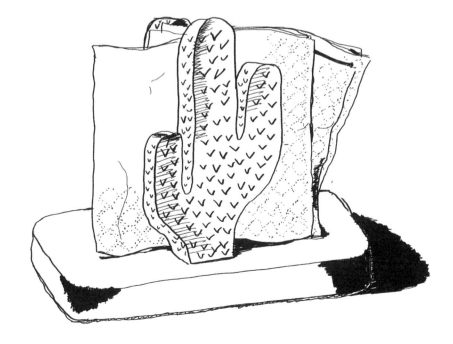

THE CREATIVE ISLAND

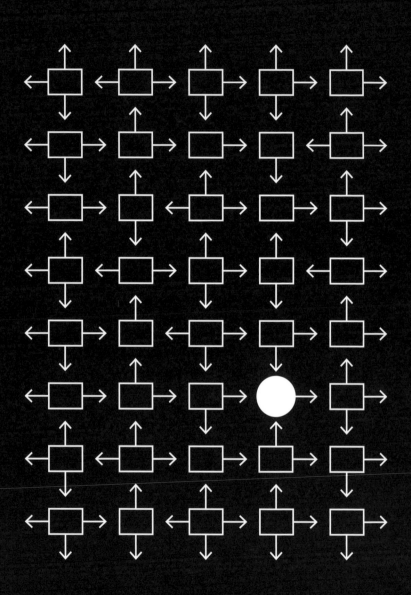

As creative people, we tend to focus on our own little creative island. But there is a whole world beyond that island, and the two influence each other. So it's smart to look outside the boundaries of what we do, as we do it.

Get yourself some data

According to designer Sophie Thomas, it is important to conduct a lifecycle analysis for a new product — even before you create a prototype. As she describes in an article published on Dezeen, a good lifecycle analysis involves a relatively long process. In it, you consider various factors such as where your materials (and other resources) come from, as well as what happens to your product at the end of its lifecycle.

Thomas gives an example: "You may be designing a chair, but the velvet you want to cover it with didn't just materialise: the farmland was mowed and fertilised; seeds were sown, cotton was watered, cut, and processed; cloth was dyed and woven; fabric was cut, packed, and delivered. And that was before you had even started the creation of the chair itself."

An endless number of green buildings doesn't make a sustainable city.

— Jan Gehl

You can make coffee by taking a capsule from a box, placing it in a machine (which will ask you to refill the water, empty the tray and then, possibly, to descale). After use, the empty capsules have to be taken away for recycling.

You can also make coffee by putting a filter with coffee in a coffee machine, adding water, and then pressing a button. Or by placing a filter with coffee on a cup and pouring hot water on it. The point of all these coffee-making methods: the simpler the process, the smaller the impact usually is — and there's less fuss involved, too.

The more complex a product is to make, the more resources you need — and usually, the greater its negative environmental impact. Take, for example, a bag made of organic cotton compared to a plastic bag from the supermarket. Plastic is less biodegradable, but the production of the cotton bag is much more complex: cotton needs a lot of water, which makes the footprint of that bag 154 times larger than that of an LDPE plastic bag. There is a footnote, though: if you use the cotton bag 155 times (and an LDPE bag only once), the cotton one is ultimately better.

So, for an eco-centred approach, you need to look beyond raw materials and how your product is produced; you need to look at the lifecycle and cost of recycling too. And then, there are always other things you could (not) do. For instance, you could encourage people to bring their own coffee cups instead of providing single-use cups.

Do you really need the coffee?

You can also start by questioning why we drink so much coffee, says bio-ethicist Dr. Sarah Chan. Do we do it to wake up? To stay sharp? For the energy kick? If that's the case, maybe we should first look at our energy management. Do we sleep enough? Do we work too much? When coffee is just a way to treat a symptom, find out what the underlying condition is.

COMPLEXITY / NEGATIVE IMPACT

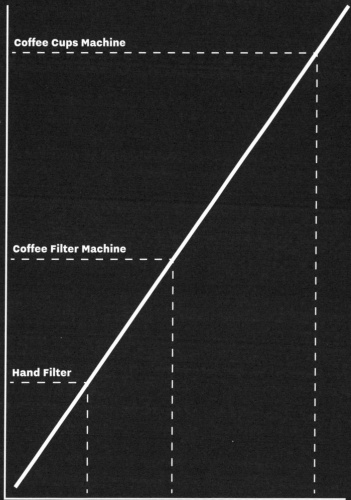

Perhaps you don't need a new coffee machine, but yoga before bedtime. And perhaps you don't need a new cotton tote bag either. You already have about 100.

> **It isn't enough just looking for quality in the products we buy, we must ensure that there is quality in the lives of the people who make them.** — Orsola De Castro

A new kid on the block

Blockchain is the technology behind crypto currencies such as Bitcoin. It is basically a decentralized ledger where each block controls the preceding block: therefore, it is a democratic vehicle. No one owns it. But each block's information always remains public and thus transparent.

Testing is currently underway on how to apply this technology to production chains. Imagine being able to scan a QR code on a product in a store and being able to check the entire supply-chain: from the T-shirt (finished product) to the cotton seeds producer.

The blockchain idea could also be applied to creative processes. In this context, everyone in the chain would only need to verify the 'block' (part of the production process) that came before them, without knowing the exact content of the 'blocks' that came before that one. Because the information from each block is public, you can basically view all production information all the way back to the beginning of the production process. This kind of decentralization of information could make it a lot harder to commit fraud. As an additional advantage, a blockchain system for creatives could also help protect copyrights and royalties.

A sidenote is that blockchain technology costs an enormous amount of energy — but new developments are expected to make it work more efficiently in the future.

If You Hack the Process

What we keep looking for is a simple way to make big changes; changes that make a substantial difference in larger systems and structures. If you know the architecture of a supply chain, you can change it — sometimes by making relatively simple choices. A practical example: if you and a few other people decide not to eat meat, that will have an effect on all parts of the meat industry chain, right down to deforestation. It is a small effect, but it's there. The same is true if you don't drive a car. The effect your choice has may be tiny, but it could inspire others to do the same, causing a ripple effect. Human see, human do.

When you create products, keep existing processes and supply chains in mind and see how you can hack them — or even change them. The choices that keep things simple are often also the ones that are least damaging to the ecosystem.

A good science fiction story should be able to predict not the automobile, but the traffic jam.

— Frederik Pohl

The term 'speculative design' was popularized by designers Fiona Raby and Anthony Dunne. Speculative design has its origins in critical design, which makes the user look differently at an object and the culture in which it was created — which in turn makes them more aware of the status quo. Speculative design is focused on the future, on possibilities and on the relationship between science, technology and humans. Its aim is to stimulate social discussion — not to design products for the market. Instead of solving symptoms, it asks questions about why we (think) we need things. It is about changing the design mindset.

Pre-analytic vision. Worldview. Paradigm. Frame. These are cousin concepts. What matters more than the one you choose to use is to realize that you have one in the first place, because then you have the power to question and change it.

— Kate Raworth

HACK THE PROCESS

Default Chain

Reversed Chain

(Re)Use What's there Chain

Repair Chain

Fewer Steps Chain

Design Backwards

When you use soap, the microplastics from that soap (because yes, it often still contains those) end up in the water. That means that contrary to what you might think, you are not the end user of the soap — everything that lives in the water is. You, the one who buys the soap and uses it in the shower, are just in the middle part of the whole process.

If you take that into consideration, it might make sense to start the production design of soap (or anything else, really) at the very end of the process — where your product ends up. That way, you're aware of the effects and thus also of what you can do to make it better. If we take the soap example, you could figure out how to make soap that causes the least possible harm, without microplastics. Or even better: you could try to find a way for the soap to do something positive for the water and everything that lives in it.

Use What's Already There

Franziska Trautmann and Max Steitz run a recycling company called Glass Half Full in New Orleans. They transform glass bottles and other glass waste back into sand. This sand is used for various purposes, including the repair of coastlines, construction and sandbags for disaster relief, as well as for the production of new glass. The glass recycling process is quite ideal because glass can be recycled without a loss of quality — which is rare. It's also relatively straightforward because glass can be easily separated from other waste materials. Glass is an exception to the rule in recycling.

Separation of materials is, in fact, the biggest challenge in recycling; you can't recycle mixed materials easily. Products are often difficult to disassemble — and it also takes too much time. If it takes minutes to remove a cap from a bottle, it becomes less worthwhile to do so.

That's why there are companies that are looking into making the disassembly of their products easier. For instance, lighting companies are designing smart click systems to avoid the need for extra materials (like screws) or additional steps (unscrewing them).

They could also just apply the ToDon't principles and leave things out. For instance, perhaps you don't need light everywhere. No light is also a form of light, just very dark — and lots of animals like it, too.

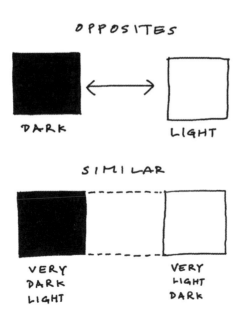

OPPOSITES

DARK ⟷ LIGHT

SIMILAR

VERY
DARK
LIGHT

VERY
LIGHT
DARK

Producing less clothing might just be the solution that the fashion industry doesn't want, but does need. As we already know, most clothes are never recycled but just dumped in a desert (see page 85). Ghana is also flooded with containers full of clothing, including 'donated' clothes from luxury fashion houses — old collections that they need to get rid of. Ghanaian designer David Kusi Boye-Doe has taken it upon himself to avoid waste and buys these clothes to use them for his own new exclusive fashion items. He creates his work with sustainability in mind, and he pays attention to social and cultural developments.

Repair by design
Manufacturers often ensure that no one but them can repair their products, and it usually costs the consumer quite a bit, too. As a result, buying new items often becomes cheaper than repairing them. Products could last longer if they could be easily repaired, also after the warranty period. But it's exactly that possibility that the manufacturers often exclude.

It's time to recognize the right to repair more fully.
— Steve Wozniak

There is a global push for the 'right to repair'. This movement wants manufacturers to design products in a way that makes them easily repairable: repairable by design. And repairs should not be exclusively done by the company itself, either. Manuals should be made publicly available, just like specialized repair tools. To encourage repair of broken products, several countries (France, Germany, Austria) subsidize the repair of various appliances, from vacuum cleaners to washing machines and smartphones.

Reuse, rebuild

According to architect Alberte Hyttel, wood is often seen as a symbol of sustainable construction, even though it is not always the most sustainable option. In fact, it can be more sustainable to reuse existing plastic materials than to use new wood.

Hyttel wants to change the symbolic use of materials. She and architect Amalie Holm create designs that call for the use of existing materials. They also try to leave the basic materials as intact as possible so that they can easily be reused. Their vision is that building materials should outlast the architecture itself. A bit like Legos.

The urban mine

Leiden University in the Netherlands is researching how we can use the city as an 'urban mine'. Why extract materials we need from polluting mines when they are already present in the city? The researchers wrote: "Raw materials from geological reserves will no longer be mined from the soil but from stocks in society." Think, for example, of (precious) metals: there are vast quantities of them in cables underground and in old smartphones and dusty laptops, but also in old ships. These ships are often sent to faraway places to be taken apart there. Why not dismantle these ships closer to home and directly reuse the materials?

Removing complexity from the production process can be achieved in various ways, often by simply taking something out. Does that involve you needing to come up with a different process? Maybe. But it also creates possibilities: creatively, financially, in terms of time, and in reducing your environmental impact. And a big plus: you might have created a more interesting product than your competitors. A quadruple win!

Remove the office

Anyone searching for the address of software company GitLab will find that they only have mailing addresses. The company, which is worth billions, doesn't have a physical office. As its website states, it is an all-remote company — and has been since its very beginning. The entire concept of having an office has been removed from their process. So, you can run an entire company without a physical building that needs heating or cooling, furniture, where electricity is used, and that people need to travel to.

Remove the cow

Not eating meat is not too hard to do for most people, but giving up cheese can be a bigger challenge. To make one kilogram of cheese, you need about 10 litres of milk, and specifically the milk protein casein, which is essential for making hard cheeses. But there are lots of problems with the dairy industry (most notably animal cruelty, greenhouse gas emissions and pressure on natural resources like water and habitats). What if we removed the dairy industry from the cheese-making process? That is what Those Vegan Cowboys actually did. They removed the cow from the process.

It wasn't easy, because it's of course the cow's body that makes the milk: it's a fermentation process that, with the help of specific bacteria, ultimately transforms grass into milk. Those Vegan Cowboys replicated and even improved this process in their lab. Now, with their 'stainless steel cow', which they named Margaret, they produce casein and whey proteins identical to those produced by cows, which they use to create cheeses. They are still working on speeding up the process, refining their techniques, and scaling up, but the concept is there: plant-based cheese that tastes just like the cheeses we've always known. It's just a matter of time until cow's milk is only for calves.

Creativity is nothing more than imagining a world that hasn't arrived yet.
— Mark Shayler

Meet cultivated meat

You will also have heard about cultivated meat. Josh Tetrick of California's Eat Just explains it this way: "Cultivated meat is real meat, but you don't have to slaughter an animal." Worldwide, more and more countries are in the process of approving cultured meat for sale to consumers. Huber's Butchery and Bistro in Singapore was one of the first restaurants to feature 'cultivated chicken' on its menu.

The larger the scale of production, the more affordable something new becomes. The first cultivated burger made by Mosa Meat cost $330,000.- to make. At Huber's, cultivated chicken pasta was on the menu for $13.70. "It looks like chicken, it smells like chicken and, what do you know, it tastes like chicken," wrote a BBC journalist.

With these new techniques, vegetarianism may soon be unnecessary. Although, perhaps the definition of what a vegetarian is will simply change.

Can you grow food without cutting down trees, without pesticides, and without watering? Yes — in the ocean.

Seaweed farms are on the rise worldwide. It's a smart crop choice because seaweed grows quickly and relatively easily. In addition, it is extremely nutritious — not only for marine life, but also for humans and other animals. Plus, seaweed is an excellent carbon dioxide sink — it removes it from the atmosphere. Often, seaweed farms also stimulate the local economies of fishing villages, where it is becoming increasingly difficult to make a living from fishing.

> **Seaweed isn't a silver bullet, but is a really important tool to work toward a better planet and more sustainable communities.**
> — Bailey Moritz

Also back on the menu are water lentils (they used to be known as duckweed but 'water lentils' just sounds better). Water lentils also grow exceptionally quickly and easily. In Southeast Asian countries, they have been consumed for a long time. In Europe, they were once eaten, too (there are water lentil recipes found in 17th-century European cookbooks), but nowadays, it's considered a 'novel food' again. Currently, applications to reintroduce water lentils to the market are under review by the European Food and Safety Authority. It might take a few more years, but things look promising according to researchers.

#8

DO MORE WITH LESS

Yes!

Ashes to Ashes

From a human perspective, a dead tree is often considered 'waste', something that needs to be cleaned up. But the natural decomposition process of a dead tree provides opportunities for many organisms. It serves as a fertile ground that enables other life and ultimately leaves no waste behind. In nature, this is generally the case: there is no waste because everything is part of the process of regeneration.

Katrina Spade is a designer and founder of Recompose, a funeral home specialized in human composting. She applied the natural cyclic principles to the way we take care of our dead and found a way to compost human bodies back into soil.

All we humans need to do is create the right environment for nature to do its job.
— Katrina Spade

Loop Biotech, founded by designers and inventors Lonneke Westhoff and Bob Hendrikx, grows fungi into coffins. When someone's remains are buried in such a coffin, they become one with nature within 45 days. Biodegradable materials like these can also be used for other purposes: mushroom bricks, for example, are twice as strong as regular bricks, but they're lighter and fully biodegradable. They also grow tremendously fast. In his TED talk, mycologist Paul Stamets shows that the possibilities of fungi and mycelium — the root structures of fungi, which can also form amazing networks — are endless.

> **I think we can make the argument that we should save the old-growth forest as a matter of national defence.** — Paul Stamets

Fabulous fungi

Fungi are impressively good recyclers. Researchers have discovered that they are able to break down polypropylene, a hard plastic that makes up 28% of our plastic waste and of which only 1% is recycled. Does that solve the plastic problem? Certainly not immediately, but it is a hopeful development.

At the same time, more techniques are being developed that enable the production of biodegradable plastics and other materials from sources like food waste. Some of those biodegradable plastics can be converted into nutrient-rich compost with the help of fungi in less than 3 months, and without harmful by-products or side-effects.

When waste is a resource

Food waste streams have become resource streams in more than one industry — and the trend keeps expanding. For example, the peels of citrus fruits or avocados can be used as raw material for 3D printed products. Can you imagine putting your old 3D printed vacuum cleaner into the compost bin at the end of its lifecycle?

Now hold that thought and combine it with the following information: all over the world, entire houses are being built through 3D-printing. A company called 14Trees built the walls of a house in just 12 hours. They built it with 70% less emissions compared to traditionally constructed houses. These printed houses also tend to be more affordable and thus accessible for people with lower incomes. And because 3D-printing is very fast, it could help address housing shortages around the world.

Imagine the impact if entire buildings were printed using waste or other biodegradable materials. This would change how houses are designed: with flexibility and affordability in mind. It would also change the big picture of urban planning.

Climate Change = Culture Change
— Ap Verheggen

Water from air

Dutch sculpture artist Ap Verheggen wondered if it was possible to create a "self-sustaining glacier in the desert". A decade of research followed, resulting in a technique that enables the production of water when off the grid — the SunGlacier project. Using solar energy and heat, the system extracts moisture from the air, condenses it, and then captures the water. A box the size of a container can extract 1,000 to 2,000 litres of water from the air in 1 day.

Now, keep that in mind while you read about the Loess Plateau. Perhaps you've seen the documentary by filmmaker and ecologist John D. Liu. He recorded how locals helped transform part of the Loess Plateau in China — a parched area that suffered greatly from erosion — into a green oasis that could produce a wealth of fruits and vegetables. As a result, erosion has been limited and the local economy received a boost. Imagine what projects like SunGlacier could do for other areas like it: increase prosperity, reduce risk of natural disasters through erosion control, and restore biodiversity.

Electricity from air...

"We are on the threshold of a gigantic revolution, based on the wireless transmission of power," wrote Nikola Tesla in the 1930s. Tesla envisioned a massive battery with the Earth at one pole and the higher atmosphere at the other pole. With this setup, he believed it would be possible to generate hygro-electricity: electricity extracted from the air via its moisture, similar to what happens when lightning is created.

In 2023, this idea was inadvertently put into practice. A team from the University of Massachusetts Amherst was working on a humidity sensor. A student had forgotten to plug it into an electrical outlet, but the device still produced an electrical signal. It turned out that the device generated a small amount of electricity from the moisture in the air, enough to power 1 pixel of a LED screen. Electricity was literally harvested from the air.

When a new energy source is discovered, critics often argue scaling up will be too difficult to make it suitable for commercial applications. Often, those critics turn out to be wrong. A start up called CascataChuva is working hard to make electricity from this source — air — suitable for mass consumption by households and companies. According to them, it will be fully recyclable and working 24/7 — which is obviously more difficult to accomplish with solar or wind power.

In 1985, Joseph Beuys produced 200 copies of 'Lemon Light/ Capri Battery'. This artwork, created on the Italian island of Capri, consisted of a yellow light bulb that Beuys had 'plugged' into a lemon and which used the lemon's energy to light up. With this piece, which he created towards the end of his life, Beuys criticised the ecological balance of human civilization.

Art is not there simply to be understood. It is more the sense of an indication or suggestion.

— Joseph Beuys

...stored in edible batteries

Meanwhile, scientists have succeeded in creating a rechargeable battery using nutrients found in common foods like almonds, nori, and capers. It's currently a prototype, but these batteries could potentially be used as sensors for medical research. The subject of the research could swallow the batteries, and once their work is done, they can be safely digested in the stomach.

Imagine these batteries being produced on a large scale. Imagine a car with a biodegradable battery. At the end of its lifespan, you just chuck it in the compost bin.

Meet the Other Crew Members

Humans have many good qualities. We excel at lots of things. There are also many things we're not so good at. Luckily, there are other crew members that can compensate for our inabilities. That's why we need to let our fellow crew members, the animals, trees and other plants, do their jobs. What if we let pigs roam (instead of eating them), rooting around and spreading seeds? They would ensure great biodiversity without us having to worry about it.

What if we protected the whales and their habitats so they could swim around their whole long lives and birth more whales? Each whale absorbs a massive amount of CO_2 — as much as 3000 trees — so a few extra whales would add up quickly.

> **Most people who bother to think about plants at all tend to regard them as the mute, immobile furniture of our world — useful enough, and generally attractive, but obviously second-class citizens in the republic of life on Earth.**
> — Stefano Mancuso

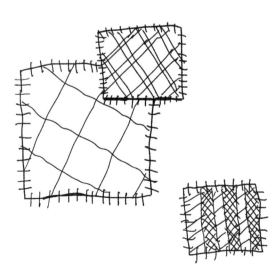

What if wild wolves hadn't been exterminated in the USA to begin with? In the early 20th century, wolves had almost completely disappeared from USA nature. Humans had simply killed most of them, and taken over their habitats. After concluding that wolves had become endangered, the USA started a recovery program. As part of that program, 41 wolves were released in Yellowstone National Park between 1995 and 1997. The wolves began to prey on deer, causing them to avoid certain areas where they were easy targets. As a result, these areas started to change: certain plants and trees returned. Birds followed, and then beavers. Beavers are excellent engineers who build dams and stabilize riverbanks, benefiting many other animals. This is how everything works together.

In 2023, ten packs were counted, and at least 108 wolves. The reintroduction of wolves was successful. But really, it would have been better to just let them live in the first place. If you don't mess with nature, you don't need to fix it either.

Speaking the language of animals

Communication is not exclusive to humans. Computer scientist Michael Bronstein uses AI to investigate the language of whales. For AI, it doesn't matter whether it looks for patterns in human language or in the language of animals. That suggests interesting possibilities. Will the next generation of humans be able to communicate with animals?

Stress is also not unique to humans. It is even found in trees and plants; they emit ultrasonic sounds when experiencing drought or being cut. Researchers have recorded these popping noises in acoustic boxes and managed to qualify them by plant type (in this case, tomato or tobacco plants) and stress type (drought or being cut). Their research also suggests that these sounds, that cannot be heard by the naked human ear, can be heard by some animals.

If I is chopping an axe into the trunk of a big tree, I is hearing a terrible sound coming from inside the heart of the tree [...] A soft moaning sound [...] It is like the sound an old man is making when he is dying slowly.

— the BFG

Fight for your right

Research has shown that animals feel pain and emotions just like we do. Why don't animals have the same rights as humans? Why do we morally accept the widespread killing of animals and the destruction of their habitats?

And what about mountains and rivers? What about land? People often claim that land belongs to them, but has the land ever been asked or received anything in return? Land, sea, plants and animals have been defenceless against humans. They can't file a complaint, because they don't have a legal identity; humans don't see them as worthy of that status. But if businesses can have a legal identity — why can't animals, plants, mountains and rivers?

As you read this, lawyers are working to obtain rights for animals, nature reserves, forests, and rivers. It has been done before: in 2017, the Whanganui River in New Zealand was the first to be granted a legal identity, similar to a human's. This means that human interaction with this river has changed fundamentally.

Imagine this becomes more common. It would have a significant impact on how we interact with nature. People could no longer see all nature, including rivers, seas, animals as resources that are just there for them to use and exploit. It would mean a completely different way of producing and living.

> **I think having land and not ruining it**
> **is the most beautiful art**
> **anybody could ever want.**
> — Andy Warhol

Symbiocene

The feeling of living at a crossroads in history is called chronocentrism — and every generation has it, including ours. Australian philosopher Glenn Albrecht is one of many who foresees a major transition in our time. According to him, we are moving from the Anthropocene to the Symbiocene or, in other words, a world of 'new companionship'. A world that no longer revolves around human existence, but around all existing life, together. As Generation Symbiocene puts it on their website, "In our industrialized world, there is a vital need for a new generation of humans working toward reintegrating human culture with the rest of life."

This idea foresees that we're moving towards a new role for humans on Earth. We go back to being the Spaceship Earth crew — no longer will we be greedy passengers fighting over the all-you-can-eat buffet. This means that we're also moving towards a completely new way of thinking and creating.

The future of design is bound up with the key role of synthesis between the various disciplines that make up the socio-economic-political matrix within which design operates... an ecological worldview could change design.

— Victor Papanek

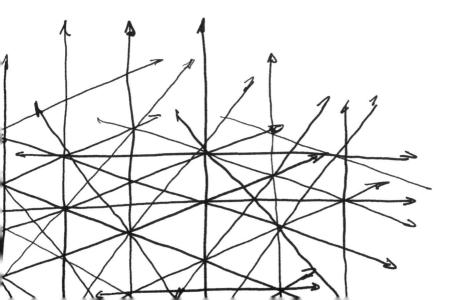

Hyperconnectivity and the Superorganism

Social scientists Anabel Quan-Haase and Barry Wellman coined the term hyperconnectivity. It refers to the high level in which people are connected via devices, platforms and social media. What's interesting is that hyperconnectivity turned out to exist in nature as well.

Ecologist Suzanne Simard discovered the 'Wood Wide Web' — the connection that tree roots have to an even larger network of fungal threads and other organisms. Through that network, trees exchange information important to the health of the entire forest, for instance information about threats like insects or drought. As humans, we are also connected to each other and the world in many ways. Just think of the 6 degrees of separation game. Or the fact that you only have to go back 10 generations to get to an ancestor at the age of the Enlightenment, and only 3 to 5 to get to an ancestor who lived through the industrial revolution.

People are much more closely connected to each other than they — than you —might think. And they are also much more connected to anything else on Earth. Ever heard of the butterfly effect? Everything is connected in ways that we cannot necessarily follow. That makes it hard to understand, which can be difficult for humans to accept.

In the 1970s, James Lovelock and Lynn Margulis developed the Gaia hypothesis, which suggests that the Earth is one giant superorganism: everything and everyone is a part of it. If you were to look at Earth from space, that theory might not feel very far-fetched.

Life on Earth is more like a verb. It repairs, maintains, re-creates, and outdoes itself.

— Lynn Margulis

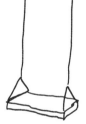

#9

STAY CONNECTED

Whatever you do, don't look away. Make sure you stay connected. Stay true to yourself; maintain connections with others, nature, and the world. It is precisely by working together that we can get a lot done.

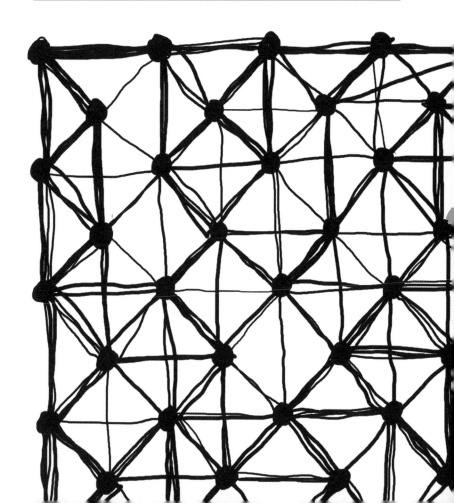

Go with the Flow

I hope that in 500 or 1000 years, when history lessons are taught about our time, they will tell the story of how we transitioned from the Anthropocene to the Symbiocene. And that it happened in less than 100 years.

We as creatives could think much more about how to reconnect with nature. I am not suggesting that we should all go back to living like cave people. We wouldn't survive that (and it would only be fun for a day or so). We could, however, be much more aware of the consequences of how we live and create.

We are all time travellers, journeying together into the future. But let us work together to make that future a place we want to visit. Be brave, be curious, be determined, overcome the odds. It can be done. — Stephen Hawking

There are multiple ways to think about solutions; no problem has only 1 dimension; and a flexible way of thinking often leads to the best outcome. When you create, create with the whole cycle in mind. And with everything around you, even the parts you cannot see.

Be ambitious; you can always raise the bar. But don't drive yourself crazy. You can't solve everything (and you don't have to), but you can change your mindset and the way you make choices — as a creative professional and as a human being.

Sometimes, you can change things by doing nothing.

ONE

The End

When I started researching this book, my goal was to create some sense of overview. Of how the world works, how it came to be that way, and what we can change about it — and how.

In my research journey, I came across all kinds of information and stories researched by people who are actually really good at that sort of thing. They wrote about history, innovation, science, politics and design. Funnily enough, I discovered that economics connects all of these fields (I used to hate economics in school).

So, here it is: Economics for Creative People. It became a collection of inspiring stories and facts that are equally shocking and inspiring. Of course, throughout the book and especially in the last chapter that looks to the future, I held on to the ToDon't principles: set boundaries, make choices, leave things out.

A Big Thank You

I would like to thank the people at BIS Publishers — specifically Harm, Anneloes, and Peter — for their trust in this third book and for their help with the production.

Another Big Thank You

I read books, interviews, blogs, articles, listened to podcasts, and watched documentaries. I want to thank all the makers, the writers, the researchers, the journalists, the scientists, the artists, and the economists for all their inspiring and important work. When you go to ToDont.co you will find a list of all the sources. Let me know if I've missed one.

The Biggest Thank You

You don't make a book on your own. Anne de Bruijn once again helped me to make this into a book. She spent uncountable hours rewriting, asking me questions, co-writing, and editing.

Dankjewel lief, ik houd van je.

FOR THE LIST OF SOURCES, LINKS, ADDITIONS, CORRECTIONS, SOCIALS, THE OTHER BOOKS, APPS, THE GAME, ETCETERA, PLEASE VISIT:

TODONT.CO

The Practice-What-You-Preach Burger

I like to eat a good burger as much as the next person. I never gave up on my Saturday Night Burger (I'm a person of habits), it's just a vegetarian one now, and it is freaking delicious.

Now, keep an open mind – it's not a 'fake meat' burger so the texture is a bit softer, but the flavour is off-the-kitchen-walls amazing. This is how you make 6 of them.

What you need:

→ **250 grams of mushrooms**
→ **1 onion**
→ **Garam masala, harissa, spicy smoked paprika powder**
→ **120 grams (wal)nuts**
→ **1 can of black beans**
→ **1 egg (or vegan alternative)**
→ **BBQ sauce/HP sauce/Worcester sauce**
→ **4 tablespoons of panko**

Recipe:

Cut 250 grams of mushrooms plus 1 onion in chunks. Fry them together in a pan with some oil at mid-level heat. Add some flavouring too: I like to use garam masala, harissa, and spicy smoked paprika powder – but you do you. Fry them for about 10 minutes, until the onions and mushrooms are browned and soft. A bonus option is to add some BBQ sauce (for that extra smoky flavour) in the last few minutes. Chuck it all in the kitchen machine and let it cool off.

In the meantime, roast a handful — about 120 grams — of coarsely chopped walnuts (or other nuts) in the dirty pan for a few minutes. Add them to the mixture and when everything has reached room temperature, add one tin of drained and rinsed black beans (about 240 grams when drained).

Add an egg (or vegan alternative), a splash of Worcester and/or HP sauce, plus a nice pinch of salt and pepper and 4 heaped tablespoons of panko. Blitz it all together, but not too long. Keep an eye on it and stop mixing when the mixture has the texture you like. If it's too dry, add some HP sauce (or alternatively ketchup). If it's too wet, add some more panko.

Divide the mixture into 6 equal portions and shape the burgers in a ring or by hand on some baking paper, and cover them with baking paper too to avoid sticking. Cool (or even better, freeze) them before use.

Fry the burgers until browned or slightly charred. When it's about done, spread some BBQ sauce on the top and flip it over. Melt a slice of good quality (vegan) cheese on the other side before transferring it to your prepped burger bun. We usually eat our burgers on toasted Turkish bread – the type often used for döner.

We like to eat our burgers with HP sauce, caramelised onions, lettuce, pickles, and jalapeños. Sometimes, we make a burger sauce out of mayo and piccalilli. Add anything you want. Or leave something out. That always guarantees something interesting.

Post your burger on Instagram and tag us!
@Bureaudonald @ACertainMissBrown

Creative Credits

Written by Donald Roos & Anne de Bruijn
Edited by Anne de Bruijn
Designed & illustrated by Donald Roos

→ Instagram **@Bureaudonald @ACertainMissBrown**

BIS Publishers

Borneostraat 80-A
1094 CP Amsterdam
The Netherlands
T +31 (0)20 515 02 30
bis@bispublishers.com
www.bispublishers.com

ISBN 978-90-636-9700-6

→ Any suggestions, questions or requests for workshops?
Please send a 5 sentence email via **ToDont.co**